WHO'S ON MY SIDE?

THE ESSENTIAL GUIDE FOR
TODAY'S RETIRED INVESTOR

Compliments of:

Thomas S. Zickau
Zickau & McCormick, LLC
545 Metro Place S., Suite 100
Dublin, Ohio 43017

866-734-8350 / 614-734-8350

tom@zickaumccormick.com
www.nwfservices.com

MIKE KASELNAK

ISBN: 0615596010
ISBN 13: 9780615596013

STORY OF A DISILLUSIONED BROKER

I BEGAN INVESTING IN THE STOCK market as a senior in high school. I continued my interest in investing during my six year tour in the US Navy in their Nuclear Power Program. After leaving the Navy, I joined corporate america for a couple of years before I finally decided to tie my vocation to my love of investing. In 1989, I landed my first job as a stockbroker with IDS Financial Services (which later became American Express Financial Corporation).

Within three-and-a-half months of joining IDS, I had become one of the top financial planning salespeople in Minnesota, and over the next two years I sold a lot of financial plans to people. But along the way, I learned something about the business of financial planning; I was becoming conflicted between my job and my clients.

While I truly believed in the planning services I provided, I felt uncomfortable with the products I offered. It wasn't that the products were bad, but I was handcuffed because I could only sell American Express products. Having already spent 15 years investing on my own, I knew there was a lot more to investing than a handful of products, and shortly thereafter my business began to drop.

In early 1991 things came to a head when my manager yelled at me for reading the Wall Street Journal. I was told that, despite the newspaper's popularity, it "was not approved reading material for American Express brokers."

It became clear to me that my suspicions about the financial business were correct. My manager didn't want me to read the Wall Street

Journal because I might learn about products we didn't offer. After all, why would anyone discourage a stockbroker from reading such an important financial newspaper? Shouldn't brokers be encouraged to broaden their exposure to the financial world?

Within two weeks of that incident, I quit my job at IDS and became an independent broker. About a year later I gave another brokerage firm a try when I was recruited by Norwest Bank in 1993 (now part of Wells Fargo). At the time, they were beginning their investment services through local branches of their bank. So rather than have clients come to my office, I traveled from branch to branch selling products and helping people all over Southeastern Minnesota. On Monday I might be around the corner from my home, but Tuesday I'd be 40 miles away, and by Wednesday I'd be almost a hundred miles away.

As you might imagine, the bank "encouraged" a transaction mentality. The system was set up in such a way that I was expected to sell stocks, bonds, and mutual funds to clients, which meant that I met with someone one time and told them which product they needed. The pressure to sell products instead of well thought out plans really started to wear on me. **But the final straw was a quota on W&F funds I had to meet each year.**

As with IDS, I became frustrated with the idea of being just a financial salesman. I left after two-and-a-half years because of the constant stress of meeting sales quotas. When I left, I had close to nine hundred clients, yet I barely knew any of the people. I knew in my heart that I wasn't really helping people as much as selling things for commissions.

In 1997, I went back to being an independent advisor and earned my CFP® designation. CFP® (Certified Financial Planner) is an independent third-party designation that brokers and advisors voluntarily work to receive in order to show their knowledge about financial planning and its ethical considerations. To earn my CFP® designation, I had to go through a comprehensive program of classes and tests, as well as take continuing education classes on a regular basis.

AN EPIPHANY

About three years into my second stint as an independent advisor, I had an epiphany. One night I was sitting at my dining room table reviewing stacks of financial information and records about my clients, and I was getting frustrated. At the time, I was subscribing to lots of financial newsletters, publications, and other investment programs to make sure I was a well-rounded and knowledgeable advisor. Yet despite my library of financial knowledge, I was pulling my hair out. Before long I was swearing, cursing, and banging my fist on the table in anger.

"What's wrong with you?" my wife asked as she entered the room. "What are you doing?"

"Here, look at this," I said as I shoved a notepad in her face. "Over the last three years I've invested $30,000 in different investment systems, newsletter subscriptions, and strategies, but if I had just taken that $30,000 and put it in the bank at 3% interest, I would have made more money than by using these systems!"

I should take a moment to explain my investment strategy. Before I'd ever put a dime of my clients' money into them, I'd research them to make sure they actually worked. But every time I became convinced that I was doing the right thing, I'd put my clients' money into them and – you guessed it – they'd stop working.

My wonderful wife, who was a psychologist at the Mayo Clinic, asked me a question that changed my life.

She asked, "Have you ever wondered if all that *supposedly* helpful information isn't rigged in the favor of the financial industry at the expense of the average investor?"

At that moment my whole world went black. In three seconds my wife had said something that I had known for years, but couldn't admit to myself. Yet once I heard it, I knew she was right.

I was faced with a difficult decision. The way I saw it I had two choices:

- I could be unethical by doing what was right for me...recommending my clients invest in managed accounts, mutual funds, and variable annuities so I could earn a commission (there was no way I would be able to live with myself if I did that).

- Or I could simply tell my clients what I had learned: Investing in things that paid me no money was best in the long-run.

As best as I could tell, I was out of business. I wasn't going to have my clients do something that I wouldn't do myself (I certainly didn't want to be putting my own money into poor investments), and telling people to do things that paid me no money was going to put me out of business. I was about to give up.

But around this time, a family member of mine had gone into a long-term care facility. Because I was an advisor, my family came to me and asked for help with my relative's financial situation. After all, I'm supposed to be an expert on finances, right?

What I found out was that I didn't know the least bit about seniors and their specific concerns. So I consulted some other advisors for their advice, and they knew just enough to be dangerous. Then I consulted some attorneys for their advice, and they also knew just enough to be dangerous. Then I consulted my accountant, and like everyone else, he knew just enough to be dangerous. So while everyone had a few ideas of what to do, no one was able to see the big picture and address everything that was involved.

As I struggled to help my family, a light bulb went on. Without realizing it, I had stumbled onto a group of individuals whose financial needs were not being addressed. And it wasn't because no one wanted to help them; the problem was that professionals like myself didn't know what was needed or how to help them.

Shortly thereafter, I revised my practice and began working solely with retired investors. I had about 350 clients at the time and kept the 35 who were 55 or older. The rest (the younger ones) I visited individually, told them what I was doing, and set them up with other brokers in town.

Over the next seven years, I continued my business, helping seniors and holding workshops to educate them. As things progressed, I became very well known throughout Minnesota as the best advisor for retired individuals because of my experience in this area.

WHY I LEFT THE BUSINESS

My business continued successfully until 2002. During these seven years, I slowly began to realize that although many brokers and advisors were serving retired investors, they were not always doing what was best for the client. Some financial professionals ignored important issues that seniors needed to address, while others were more concerned with selling products to retired investors than actually helping them. I started spending more and more time specifically addressing all the things other advisors forgot which, unfortunately, was a significant portion of what seniors needed to protect themselves and their families.

I learned that the vast majority of advisors and brokers were more concerned about selling investments and products than catering to the needs of their clients. And because of this lack of experience, or "selling at all cost mentality," many clients in my area left their advisors and asked me to help them with their financial affairs.

It wasn't long before many of my fellow brokers and advisors complained about me. In fact, some of them complained to the Certified

Financial Planner Board of Standards, the organization responsible for the CFP® designation.

When problems arose between the board of Certified Financial Planners and me, the Board set up a phone appointment to discuss the situation. During the meeting, I was chastised for taking clients away from fellow professionals. I responded by insisting that I would never pull clients away from another financial professional.

"You're doing it on a regular basis," the board told me. "You're pulling approximately a hundred clients away from professionals in your area every single year."

I insisted that this wasn't the case. "What do you mean?" they asked me as they started naming names of brokers that had lost clients to me.

"That's my point, I don't consider financial sales people to be professionals" I said. "People left their brokers to come to me because those CFP® brokers weren't acting like financial professionals. Shouldn't financial professionals help their clients make sure they have the correct beneficiaries on all their investments? Shouldn't they be helping clients reduce their taxes as much as legally possible? Shouldn't they be making sure that their clients are getting the highest return possible with the least amount of risk?"

I further explained myself, "None of these people came to me because of a product that I offer. They left their advisors and came to me because I was handling things other brokers either didn't know how to do or didn't want to take the time to do."

By the end of our meeting, the CFP Board still had a problem with me taking so many clients from other CFP's in my town. We agreed to disagree and left the matter at that.

Less than two months later, I saw that Suze Orman, the well-known financial author, columnist, and guru was having the same problem with the CFP Board. Suze (a CFP® like myself) was being threatened with discipline for using what the board considered to be derisive language about brokers.

Yet Suze was doing much the same thing I was, saying that clients needed to work with someone who cared about them, not someone who was concerned about the size of their commission check. And Suze emphasized that selling a product does not demonstrate caring. Selling a product demonstrates that someone cares about their own pocketbook, rather than their client.

So after a year of watching the investment world deteriorate and continue to ignore the needs of investors, I decided to leave the business. Evidence of a crumbling of standard in the financial world was the CFP Board's decision to allow a few firms with a lot of clout to give their brokers "lite" versions of the CFP® designation. Many members left in anger at what they considered to be watering down of the designation.

I was one of those members, and I decided to retire my CFP® designation because I believed their actions were not always in the best interests of clients or the profession. Two thousand and two was the same year that Wall Street greed and fraud became daily news across the country. There were fraud issues with several mutual fund companies. Corporate executives like Dennis Kozlowski of Tyco were on trial for stealing corporate funds, and investor confidence in the financial industry was at an all-time low. Little did I know this was just the beginning; two thousand and eight would see a near collapse of the banking and financial industry as a result of Wall Street's lack of transparency.

I was angry and disappointed with what the financial services industry had become and decided that the best thing I could do was to leave the industry and use my knowledge to help people who had retired to protect their years of hard work and effort.

I hope you'll agree that I made the right decision.

CHAPTER 1

ABOUT THE HANDBOOK

UILDING UPON MY EXPERIENCE, I'VE written this book to help you, the senior investor, learn what your financial advisor should be doing to look out for your best interests. Whether it's IRAs, long-term care insurance, or setting your portfolios up to draw the most income possible without worry of running out of money... you need to know what to expect from your advisor. And if this book teaches you that your current advisor isn't giving you the help you deserve, I'll teach you how to find one who will.

But it's important to remember one thing. You should never act on the ideas in this book alone. I can't emphasize this enough. This book is designed to help you find the best advisor for you, not to replace your advisor. In absolutely no way am I suggesting that you fire your advisor if he or she has been doing his or her job, or that you start handling your investments alone. Being your own advisor is great, as long as you hold yourself to the same standards as a professional. So don't put these ideas to use before you consult with a competent advisor who specializes in working with people who are retired.

What do I mean by this?

A good advisor that specializes in working with people who are retired must be "current" in certain areas:

- IRS tax law as it pertains to all Retirement Plans

- Issues pertaining to Social Security Income and planning

- New Income Planning techniques that work with any investment

- Probability and random-nature theory (risk management)

In fact, while reading this book, if you come across something that you want to know more about or need to fix in your own portfolio, make a note of it and call an advisor. Run these ideas by him or her, and get his or her advice. Be sure to ask questions and decide for yourself if their advice is appropriate for you.

Above all, I want this book to help you become an informed consumer. My hope is it will be a valuable resource for you to help you improve your financial situation.

THE ESSENTIAL FINANCIAL HANDBOOK

As we all know, one of the great things about the United States is that anyone who works hard, saves their money, and takes care of themselves is able to achieve the American Dream. But unfortunately, we also know that there are people always grabbing at your piece of the American Dream; those people are Uncle Sam, big banks, and Wall Street.

As an example, everyone pays taxes...and almost all of us insist we pay too much. A lot of people ask, "Why should someone who has worked hard and saved their money their whole life have to pay more than someone who is lazy?" In fact, I'm willing to bet that you agree.

Well, I have good news and bad news. The bad news is that you probably *are* paying too much in taxes.

I'm often asked which political party would be better for the economy and taxes: Democrats or Republicans? I don't have an answer. The only thing we can be certain of is the nature of politicians.

If we analyze the word politics, we find it is made up of two Greek root words: "Poli" and "tic". "Poli" means many, and "tic" is a parasitic blood sucker...so no matter who gets into office, we can be certain they will always find a way to take our money.

The good news is that this book will help you learn how to stop paying so much in taxes and protect yourself from Wall Street antics.

Let's take a quick look at some of the other things we will discuss:

- **Income:** How to increase your income AND decrease your chances of running out of money. Impossible? You'll find out it's both possible and easy.

- **Taxes:** We'll look at income taxes, Social Security taxes, and even estate taxes throughout the book. In fact, you may not realize it, but even the money and investments you leave behind for your family will be taxed. So we'll spend some time discussing how to minimize the taxes associated with your inheritance.

- **Long-Term Care:** Long Term Care is a growing area of concern for seniors, and we'll look at the 10 secrets your advisor doesn't want you to know about LTC.

- **Probate:** You'll also find out the dirty little secret about how banks and brokers profit from your probate, and how to bypass them completely.

- **Advisors:** This is perhaps the most important topic of this book. If you follow the news, you know that there seems to be a constant stream of lawsuits filed against investment bankers, analysts, and stockbrokers. Most of these lawsuits have to do with fraud perpetrated against investors like you. Are they all out to cheat you and steal your money? You'll learn how to protect yourself from unethical advisors who care more about lining their own pockets than about your investments.

When you get down to it, there are really four fundamental realities to investing:

1. Reduce your taxes

2. Beware of unethical stockbrokers and insurance agents

3. Achieve your investment goals with the least amount of risk.

4. Create an income stream that you cannot outlive.

These have always been important. But since 2008, mastering these issues has become vital (this book will address all of these things).

Like many retired investors, you've accumulated a lot of wealth over the last 40 years, and it's important to learn how to preserve it. The last thing anyone wants is for their life savings to disappear because of a bad decision...and the information I'm going to share with you will help you avoid costly mistakes.

When Justice Learned Hand, one of the greatest Appellate Court justices in our country's history, made the above statement, he meant that the uninformed people of the United States usually pay more in taxes than those who are informed. However, keep in mind that informed people who do not act on their knowledge are no better off than those who are uninformed. So if you want to increase your income, reduce your taxes, and avoid unethical stockbrokers, it's not enough to simply read this book. In order for the advice in this book to be of any benefit, you'll need to act upon what you learn.

> "There are two systems of taxation in our country: one for the informed and one for the uninformed."
>
> *-JUSTICE LEARNED HAND,*
> *UNITED STATES APPELLATE COURT.*

LEARNING FROM THE U.S. NAVY

Whenever Navy ships come into port, they always test the ship's anchor chains. If you've ever seen a U.S. Navy ship at port, you've probably noticed that the anchor is attached to the ship by a huge chain with links of steel that are well over five inches thick.

Why, then, are the chains tested each time the ships dock in port? Surely those chains never break, and no sailor who has been at sea wants to spend time testing each link of such a huge chain when they are about to set foot on shore for the first time in months.

But the Navy requires this kind of testing because the Navy needs to find any problems with the chain *before* it breaks. It's called a stress test. It's almost always a good idea in any situation – especially investing.

My point is that you should always find out if something has problems before the problems arise. The same holds true for investing:

- If you hold technology stocks, when do you want to find out if they might be worthless? Now or in two years when the company goes bankrupt?

- If you have Long Term Care insurance, when do you want to find out about potential problems with your coverage...now or once you're in a nursing home?

- If there is a chance of running out of money, do you want to fix it now or wait until it's too late?

- If you've mistakenly disinherited your grandchildren, would you like to know about it now (when it can be fixed) or let it go and hope that everything works out after you are gone?

Stress tests make sure that everything in your portfolio and financial documents has been taken care of before it's too late. We'll give you several stress tests for several areas of your finances throughout this book.

CHAPTER 2

THE GREATEST GENERATION

A S RETIRED INVESTORS, THERE IS no question that you've worked long and hard for everything you have. Your generation built this country. You built the United States into the most powerful nation in the world. You built communities, businesses, and a strong government while also developing the sciences and the arts. You put a man on the moon, invented the internet, and provided women the opportunity to enter the workforce.

More importantly, your sacrifices and hard work changed the course of American history. And through it all, you never complained.

Yet today, as grandparents and retirees, how are you rewarded for your years of struggle and hard work? By paying high taxes? By supporting people who have just moved to this country, yet have never paid a single dollar into the system?

If you become sick and need to be hospitalized in a long-term care facility for an extended period of time, who pays for it? You do, of course. And just how long are you expected to pay for your stay? Until you're broke.

Compare that to many of our nation's policies on health care for the uninsured and immigrants and you are likely to become angry. For example, if a brand new immigrant moves to the United States, then becomes ill and needs hospitalization, do they pay for it? Of course not! Government programs pay for their medical needs, and taxpayers like you fund these programs.

This is not to say that immigrants should not receive medical assistance or that we should turn these people away. In fact, one of the great things about your generation is that you've encouraged people across the world to come here, work hard, and achieve the same success you had.

But...you should not be treated so unfairly.

You've paid your dues to this country. You've given the United States your hard work and sweat for more than 40 years. But once you need help, the government does nothing until you are broke.

It doesn't exactly seem fair, does it?

THE RULES OF THE GAME

When situations like this occur, we often believe that other people get special treatment; that we're missing out on something because we play by the rules. We may feel helpless, forced to stand by and watch while others cheat to get what they want.

In the real world, cheaters eventually get caught. We hear about people who falsify medical information in order to qualify for treatments or surgeries. Executives and firms on Wall Street get fined because they're caught cheating investors. People like Ken Lay at Enron and Bernie Madoff are held personally accountable for using their companies as a personal piggy bank. And don't even get me started on the big banks, their executives and their million dollar bonuses.

But how are they punished? Are they required to return the billions they've stolen from middle-income America? Not hardly. They get a few years in a country club prison, but the billions they stole are gone forever.

Then there are those people who don't cheat, but they seem to get special treatment as they get ahead. Why do they get special treatment? Because they know the rules of the game. Whether it's taxes, investing, or your finances, some people are able to take advantage of situations because they know the rules. You may be stuck watching people get ahead because there are rules you don't understand or don't even know about.

Have you ever played a game with someone where you didn't know all the rules, but the other person knew them inside and out? Who won? Most likely, they did – and not because they cheated. They just knew the rules better than you.

When it comes to taxes, investing, and your finances, there are a lot of rules out there you may not even be aware of. This book is going to make sure you know and understand some of these rules. However, it is up to you to use them if you want to get ahead. Trust me; the rulebook can work in your favor if you use it to your advantage.

AN INFORMED CONSUMER

This book is also going to discuss a wide variety of topics in several areas. While you have already been given an overview of these things, it is in no way comprehensive. Actually, any of the topics we are going to discuss could probably be a book by itself.

But remember that no book can determine what is important to you right now. Income, protecting yourself from running out of money, IRAs, municipal bonds, long-term care – your situation is unique to you and your family. Some topics will be more important to you than others. The important thing is that you make notes as you read these chapters, and ask your qualified senior advisor about these topics the next time you speak with him or her.

CHAPTER 3

WHEN DID THE FINANCIAL SERVICES INDUSTRY GO SO WRONG?

BEFORE WE DISCUSS THE NUTS and bolts of financial planning, it's necessary to understand where the retired investor fits into the financial planning community as a whole. After all, you can't accurately know what to expect from your advisor, if you don't understand how you are viewed by the financial services industry.

A QUICK HISTORY OF FINANCIAL PLANNING

The financial services industry may have been around for years, but the idea of financial planning is relatively new by comparison. And for our purposes (as well as your best interests) you need to think about financial services as financial planning.

Stockbrokers have been selling products since before J.P. Morgan made his first million. Wall Street has a long and interesting history, most of which has been dedicated to making the wealthy...wealthier.

Financial planning is a relatively recent addition to the financial industry. Unlike the traditional model of stockbrokers (who sell products to anyone who would buy them for a commission), financial planning requires that an advisor look at the whole picture of their client's financial situation. They help them solve any of a variety of issues they may face (If you remember my personal history from the Introduction, you'll see how I evolved from a traditional stockbroker to a financial planner in my own career.)

The concept of financial planning really began in the 1970's with American Express, Vanguard, and Fidelity. These firms began to see the value in not just selling investments, but helping clients select the right investment for their needs. Financial planning eventually grew to include complementary services (like estate planning and tax advice) in order to meet the growing needs of clients. No longer was it good enough to simply sell a product to a client. Advisors were now interested in their clients' financial goals (like buying a new home or sending their kids to college), as well as capital gains, tax implications, and other issues that were impacting their investments.

As the years went on, the concept of financial planning became more accepted by the general public. As investors realized the value of this service, they grew to demand more from their stockbroker than a list of products and a sales pitch. The increased demand caused major Wall Street investment banks to begin offering their own version of financial planning. Soon, companies like Merrill Lynch and Piper Jaffray (now part of UBS) had jumped on the bandwagon, touting financial plans as the new evolution in financial services in order to remain competitive and keep clients.

Today, financial planning has become an integral part of the financial services industry. No matter where you go (be it a wirehouse, a regional firm, or an independent advisor), financial planning is now an expected part of an advisor's job. Yet, as we will discuss in a later chapter, not all financial planners are created equal.

FINANCIAL PLANNING FOR THE RETIRED

We all need different things at different times in our lives, and this applies to our finances as well. So it should come as no surprise that retired folks need a different kind of financial planning than other investors.

Think about it. Do you have the same debt problems that your children have? Maybe...maybe not. You may owe a few thousand dollars on a car loan or a hospital bill, but your children are still paying off college...as well as thousands of dollars in credit card debt, if they're like most working folks.

Do you have the same investment problems that your children have? Probably not. Your concern is producing enough income and holding onto the money you have so you can enjoy your retirement and eliminate the worry of running out of money. Your children, on the other hand, are desperately trying to save enough so they can afford to retire (not to mention saving for their own children's college education).

Do you have the same health problems that your children have? Probably not. You may have existing conditions that require hundreds or thousands of dollars of medications each year, as well as expensive medical treatments and specialists. Maintaining the human body is not cheap. Your kids (now in their 30's and 40's) are just now beginning to have occasional health problems as their eyes start to deteriorate and the occasional back pain becomes more common.

Your finances have nothing in common with your children. So why compare your investments and financial situation to your children and others who are at different stages in their lives and need different things from their money? The fact is that you shouldn't.

Unlike most financial plans that focus on making more money, senior planning:

- Shows you how to keep what you have to produce enough income to live comfortably
- Helps you avoid paying unnecessary taxes.

An advisor who specializes in your planning should be willing to review your taxes, your income plan, your beneficiaries and titling, your catastrophic protection, and your legal affairs...all on an annual basis. How many run-of-the-mill advisors do that?

Yet retired folks are told they should continue to think and invest like everyone else.

When I ask seniors how they are doing financially, most say "Great! I made 'this much' last year," or "Terrible! I lost 'this much' last year."

But does it really matter how much money you made last year? No, what matters is how much income you can withdraw without fear of running out of money.

You realize that you are no longer putting money away...you did that all your working lives. You are in a place in your life that you want to spend your money without fear of running out. That's the essence of planning for people that are retired.

Don't believe me? Well, let's say that you had a huge rate of return last year. Would you go buy a yacht? How about a vacation home? Would it change your lifestyle at all?

On the other hand, what if you ended up giving two-thirds of that huge return back to Uncle Sam in taxes? Or it's unexpectedly eaten up by health care bills. Or your affairs are so jumbled up and are such a mess that once you die, your spouse doesn't understand anything and makes some bad decisions?

These are all very real examples of the financial problems people like you face every day. If you want to avoid these kinds of issues, you need to stop planning your finances as if you were fresh out of college and start planning your finances to reflect the concerns you have today. Trust me, you'll thank me later.

And because of your unique situation, you and every other retired investor in the country should have an advisor who understands your unique situation and can cater to your investment needs. Just as some financial advisors cater to the ultra-wealthy and specialize in helping multi-millionaires manage their money, there are advisors who are trained to specifically handle the needs of seniors like you. And if the AARP can make Capitol Hill cater to the needs of seniors, shouldn't advisors do the same?

THE GOOD AND THE BAD

As with everything, there are some great things about the current world of financial planning and some problems you need to be mindful of.

The good news is that most Financial Advisors are likely to be independent advisors. This means there will be less conflict of interest and a wider range of options available to you. If you recall my own personal experience, I realized how difficult it is to do what is best for a client when you're only able to offer your firm's proprietary products and services.

Independent advisors, on the other hand, have the freedom to offer products and services they truly believe in without any pressure from an employing firm. One of the good developments in the financial planning arena is that many financial planners have left the big Brokerage Houses and firms to become independent. Most advisors do this because they want to do what is right for their clients. Fortunately, this trend continues to this day.

Now the bad news: Core beliefs behind financial planning are deteriorating as more and more brokers jump on the financial planning bandwagon. You've already heard my opinions about the CFP Board and how that once great organization has caused controversy among planners like me.

Many professionals believe that the CFP Board has lost its moral compass and that by allowing wirehouses to freely give out the CFP® designation, the standards behind the certification are rapidly dropping. So while such designations as these are intended to represent an advisor's knowledge and ethics, you should rely on your own intuition as to whether or not your advisor has your best interests at heart. Beware of the alphabet soup syndrome. Just because an advisor has some letter behind his name does not necessary make him trustworthy. It's a start, but you should dig a little deeper.

Now that you've got a better understanding of what financial planning is all about, let's take a look at Wall Street and why investors like you have been treated so badly.

HOW DID THIS HAPPEN?

Wall Street has never been easy to understand, but in recent years the road for investors has gotten even rockier. It's hard enough to decide where to put your money when the market is doing well, but these days it's a whole different ballgame. Company earnings announcements are more complicated than the IRS tax code. The difference between comparable mutual funds is like splitting hairs. As if that's not enough, investors now have to contend with a landslide of recent corporate scandals. Not surprisingly, just planning for your retirement in the 21st Century is akin to walking through a minefield.

Corporate greed made headlines back in the 1980's thanks to Michael Milken, junk bonds, and the movie "Wall Street". The general public's skepticism towards Wall Street was at an all-time high, and watching actor Michael Douglas portray a greedy investment tycoon confirmed our opinions. When the character, Gordon Gekko, told a roomful of stockbrokers that "Greed is good," our distrust of the financial services industry was solidified.

But once the roaring 80's ended, the market took a turn for the worse. Everyone, including the Gordon Gekkos of the world, began losing money. Investors had more important things to worry about than whether or not their stockbroker was a sleazy salesman cheating them out of better returns.

Eventually, the frustration of the early 1990's gave way to the dot-com boom. On the eve of a new millennium, we watched our economy grow faster than it ever had, transformed by technology and a new form of communication called the Internet. No longer was the future about flying cars and trips to outer space. The future had arrived, and it was about connectivity, speed, and the ability to see or do anything at the click of a button.

Wall Street took notice by investing in the phenomenon heavily and rapidly. Twenty-something's who were running websites out of their parent's basements were given millions of dollars based on nothing more than a vague plan and a few computers. And for a while, it worked. Everyone owned Internet and technology stocks, and we considered taking our money out of tried-and-true successes like the S&P 500 because some new company with a name we couldn't spell was seeing quarterly double-digit earnings.

But as we all know: anything that looks too good to be true probably is. And, of course, this was the case with the dot-com boom of the late 90's. Common sense finally came back to Wall Street, and once investors realized that most of these Internet companies were never going to be profitable, we cut our losses and regained our wits.

Unfortunately, it wasn't just investors who were swayed by the excitement of this period. Companies and financial firms alike expected to see huge profits and growth, and many of them would do anything to get them. So while many of us lost our shirts when the bubble burst, some corporations weren't willing to admit they'd done the same. Rather than admit their mistakes, they began a dangerous charade – one where the company pretended to be profitable while executives stole money and left investors, such as you, footing the bill.

ENRON: A TALE OF LIES AND COVER-UPS

At the beginning of 1991, Enron was an example of corporate success and a stock sought after by investors. The company's profits continued to rise quarter after quarter, and its executives lived like kings.

But by December of that year, everything had changed. Enron had declared bankruptcy, creating the biggest corporate collapse in American history. As a result, many investors and employees were left broke. A vice chairman committed suicide. Arthur Andersen, the energy giant's accounting firm went under because it had looked the other way while executives used corporate expense accounts for everything from personal cell phones to trips to adult clubs.

Enron became successful because it took advantage of utility deregulation in the late 80's. At the time, users were allowed to buy gas or electricity from any number of producers, and the company made a lot of its money by selling contracts to deliver natural gas and other forms of energy in the future. But in August 2001, chief-executive-officer Jeffrey

Skilling abruptly left the company, leaving investors and analysts worried. Soon the company's stock price began to drop even though its chairman, Kenneth Lay, insisted things were fine.

That October, the company set aside $35 million to reflect losses from two partnerships. As investors, regulators, and the general public began to ask questions, it was discovered that the partnerships had been set up in 1999 to conceal the corporation's overwhelming debt. Once the truth came to light, Enron was forced to restate and "correct" its numbers, which resulted in a $1.2 billion loss in equity. Shareholders of Enron saw their investments fall through the floor, and the company's stock spiraled downward.

Investigators discovered that not only were Enron executives using corporate funds for personal purchases and expenses, but that they also had been covering their tracks for years. Arthur Andersen, the company's auditor, was also raked over the coals for destroying documents and taking part in the charade. As a result of this mess, Arthur Andersen was found guilty of obstructing justice and has been defunct in the United States ever since.

Enron executives such as Kenneth Lay were under investigation and indictment for conspiracy and fraud charges, and many employees of the corporation watched their retirement funds disappear. (As an aside: Kenneth Lay never served a day in prison for his involvement in Enron's downfall. He died while on vacation three months before his sentence was scheduled to begin).

Sadly, while Enron has been the most significant example of corporate greed in recent years, it is far from an isolated incident. Other companies such as Global Crossing and WorldCom declared bankruptcy around the same time, and even Wall Street firms such as JP Morgan Chase and Citigroup were tarnished by their involvement in the scandal. In 2003, the two investment banks agreed to pay a combined $255 million to settle charges that they helped Enron commit fraud.

WHAT ABOUT BROKERAGE FIRMS AND MUTUAL FUNDS?

Of course, we can look at Enron and tell ourselves, "That's just one company. At least my mutual funds are diverse enough to help soften the damage any one company might make to my portfolio."

Even though that makes sense, it's a dangerous assumption. By not putting all our eggs in one basket, we lull ourselves into a false sense of security, thinking that we'll be immune from any scandals. Sadly, it's just not true.

It was hard enough when investors realized that some corporations had acted unethically and lied to investors to make money. But just when it seemed corporate accountability was starting to improve, the mutual fund industry was shaken by a scandal in late 2003.

In September of that year, New York Attorney General Eliott Spitzer settled with the hedge fund company Canary Capital on charges regarding mutual fund trading abuses. During the investigation and settlement, four additional fund companies, Janus Capital, Strong Financial, Bank of America, and Bank One, were also implicated.

Before long, things began to steamroll as Spitzer and the Securities and Exchange Commission (SEC) found that these companies weren't the only ones breaking the rules. By November, over 20 companies were involved in the scandal, including such Wall Street heavyweights as Bear Stearns, Merrill Lynch, Smith Barney, UBS, Wachovia, and Morgan Stanley. In fact, that same month, Morgan Stanley agreed to pay $50 million to settle charges that the brokerage firm did not tell investors that it was receiving compensation for selling certain mutual funds.

Mutual Fund Myths

● **Funds are long-term investments.**

424 funds disappeared in 2002, and 24% of funds that existed in 1986 are now gone.

- Managers have the discipline to hold long-term.

Turnover rates have climbed from 15-20% in 1950 to an average of 85% today.

- Fund costs are declining as they grow in size.

On average, fund costs have doubled.

This kind of revenue sharing, which happens when mutual fund companies pay kickbacks to brokerages for encouraging investors to buy their funds, was happening all over the place. Following Spitzer's lead, the SEC announced that the act was "common practice" after conducting its own investigation of the mutual fund industry. According to the SEC, about half of the brokerages they targeted paid their stockbrokers extra money when they sold shares of these particular funds.

Essentially, these companies were making trades that caused individual investors such as you to lose money. These companies were doing something called "late trading." This is when investors illegally buy or sell shares after the market's close, but still get the closing price. Mutual funds are priced once a day at the close of the market, and orders placed after that time are supposed to use the next day's closing price.

This may not sound like a big deal, but if important news is announced after the market closes, these late traders were almost guaranteed a profit, or at least avoided a loss.

Why is this a big deal? Well, besides the fact that it was illegal, these companies were taking other people's profits!

Let's say a mutual fund with $500 million grows an additional $10 million during a day of trading. Now, let's say that a hedge fund invested an additional $50 million in late trading, and that they got that day's price. Instead of the $10 million in profit being spread among the original $500 million, it's now spread among $550 million – which means that investors like you get a smaller piece of profit, while a company that hadn't even invested in the fund makes a huge return.

Not surprisingly, the fallout from all this scheme was pretty significant. Lawrence Lasser, the CEO of Putnam Investments, lost his job, as did Richard Strong, CEO of Strong Financial. In fact, the scandal even impacted the SEC. During the investigation, the head of the SEC's Boston office resigned because he knew about some of these companies' activities, but looked the other way.

WHAT SHOULD I DO?

Even the "gold standards" of the mutual fund industry (Fidelity, Vanguard, and American Funds) had been found to be involved in some of these shady practices, so few mutual fund investors remained unscathed.

And looking at the brokerage side of the scandal, just about every major wirehouse in the country was involved in some way. So even though your broker may have been an upstanding person, he or she couldn'tspeak for his or her whole firm.

The bottom line is that there isn't any need to completely avoid mutual funds (or individual stocks) because of what has happened. But you should learn from these scandals and make sure that nothing you own – bonds, stocks or mutual funds – is involved in any shady practices. How can you be sure? You can start by having a financial advisor whom you trust review your investments for these issues.

WILL THINGS CHANGE?

While these scandals have certainly rocked Wall Street, they don't mean the stock market is nothing but gamblers and cheaters. There are still great, ethical companies that make money for their shareholders and plenty of funds that haven't been involved in any wrongdoing.

However, as we've said in previous chapters, retired investors aren't in the accumulation phase of their investing lives, and these kinds of events can be catastrophic.

Keep your eyes open, ask lots of questions, and you should be just fine. Sadly, these kinds of scandals aren't going to stop. After all, Wall Street has always attracted more than its fair share of crooks; that's not going to change. No one can predict the future, but you can make sure your chances of

> But, sadly these kinds of scandals aren't going to stop. After all, Wall Street has always attracted more than its fair share of crooks....

being involved in a future scandal are minimized. Find an advisor who has your best interests in mind. The best way to do that is to follow the advice in the next chapter.

In the next chapter you will learn how to pick a good advisor, what to look for, and things to keep in mind as you evaluate your current financial professional.

CHAPTER 4

USE AN ADVISOR OR DO-IT-YOURSELF?

L IKE MANY RETIRED INVESTORS, YOU are probably using some sort of financial advisor. You may be working with a broker, an insurance agent, a mutual fund salesperson, a CD or savings account specialist at the bank, or an accountant. And like many financial consultants, they may call themselves an advisor. But are they?

The Merriam-Webster dictionary defines an advisor as "someone who provides counsel, as well as warnings, recommendations, and concerns." It also defines an advisor as "someone who provides information." In other words, a true advisor gives you his or her informed and knowledgeable opinion, along with warnings about risks and consequences.

In the world of financial advice, an advisor is someone who gives guidance based on both existing and predicted conditions. For example, taxes are an existing and ongoing condition that your advisor should be able to provide advice on. Also, things like the possibility of needing additional income while at the same time eliminating your chance of running out of money should be discussed. Your advisor should be able to provide information about these kinds of things, as well as spell out potential benefits and potential risk to you and your family.

Do I Need a New Advisor?

One of the most important things you can do is ask yourself the following: "Am I using an advisor, or am I working with a salesperson?"

If you aren't sure, look at your concerns and financial plans for the future. Is your current advisor giving you advice and options about the topics that are important to you?

If you hear about techniques that could put you in a better position, but your financial professional has never told you about them, there are two possible explanations. Either your advisor doesn't know about them, or he or she simply doesn't care. Of course, neither answer is one you want to hear.

Has your advisor set up a detailed, year-by-year income plan for you? It should project at least 10 years into the future and take market ups and downs into account.

There are certain things you should expect from your advisor, and here is a general list to help you think about your current financial advisor.

- **Integrity:** It's essential that you trust your advisor. An advisor with integrity takes his or her responsibilities and your expectations seriously and knows that principles are more important than his or her own personal gain.

- **Connectivity:** Your advisor should be part of a network or group whose sole mission is to put your goals and needs first.

This group would be able to pool their experience, expertise, and knowledge for your benefit.

- **Objectivity:** Every recommendation your advisor makes should be based solely on what is best for you. He or she should not suggest products or services that don't meet your needs or financial goals. Good advisors use their experience and knowledge to carefully consider your situation, then provide advice based on what will best meet your goals.

- **Competency:** Your advisor should be knowledgeable about the products or services he or she recommends and offers. More importantly, your advisor should never offer advice about products or services he or she isn't qualified and licensed to provide. Advisors who do so are breaking the law.

- **Privacy:** You give your advisor personal information about your financial status, as well as other personal information. In return, your advisor should not share this information with anyone else, unless you give him or her permission to do so when conducting business on your behalf. The only exception to this would be if your advisor was ordered by a court of law to provide this information.

Whether or not you need a new advisor is a question you will have to answer yourself. But trust your instincts. As a paid professional, your advisor should be able to completely explain and address every aspect of your financial concerns. If not, you may need to consider looking for someone else.

WHAT CONSUMER REPORTS FOUND

In January 1998, Consumer Reports ran a report in their magazine about a secret shopper who went to several financial advisors.

Now, if you aren't familiar, a secret shopper is someone who pretends to be a normal shopper, but records everything that goes on. After visiting the businesses, the shopper then writes a report about their findings and compares how the companies treat consumers.

In this report, the secret shopper went to five advisors; one with American Express (Ameriprise), one with Merrill Lynch, one with Prudential Securities, and two independent advisors. The shopper found that two of those five advisors were superior to the others. Which advisors do you think came out on top?

Yep, it was the independent advisors. But why do you think this was the case?

The shopper went on to explain that only the two independent advisors addressed all of his goals. He also said that while all the finished plans looked slick and professional, the other advisors recommended products that came from their own company.

It's not surprising. Talk to anyone who invests with Merrill Lynch, and they are likely to own Merrill Lynch mutual funds. Ask someone who invests with American Express (Ameriprise) the same question, and they will probably say they have Ameriprise products in their portfolio. Advisors do this because it's good for business... plain and simple. Well, of course it's good for their business, but that doesn't necessarily mean it's good for yours.

WHO DO THEY WORK FOR?

Let's say you've decided to buy your grandson a car for his birthday. You've also decided that it needs to be safe and reliable and get good gas mileage. So you go to your local Nissan dealership and tell the salesperson that you want a reliable, economical car that gets good gas mileage.

"Oh, sure," he tells you, "You should test drive a Toyota Tercel! The dealership is just down the street on the left."

Is that what the salesperson would say to you? No, not likely. The Nissan salesperson wouldn't recommend a Toyota, or a Honda, or any other type of car because it would be bad for business. How would a car salesperson make any money if he or she recommended cars that weren't on his or her lot, even if another brand was better for you?

Now apply that logic to advisors. Why do you think advisors with a big firm or wirehouse recommend that you buy their fund? Is it possible that out of 7,581 mutual funds[1], theirs just happens to be the best? It's possible, but the odds certainly aren't in their favor. Like the car salesperson, advisors do this so they and their firms can make more money, and the term for these biased recommendations is selling from a "preferred list."

Have you ever tried to move proprietary investments...things like Merill Lynch mutual fund or an Ameriprise annuity...from one firm to another? It isn't possible. It doesn't matter what firms you are talking about; you can't say, "Well, I'd like to take $10,000 in proprietary funds out of my portfolio and move it over to my account at this other firm." You can't even get these firms to move your funds to accounts you might have with independent advisors. The bottom line is that firms that have you invested in their funds will not let you move them out of their firm without big penalty charges and taxes.

Simply put, these firms have you handcuffed to their products and services. If you do move, you are hit with all kinds of charges and fees like a slap on the wrist. If you own B shares, there are surrender charges and possible taxes. So if you have a proprietary mutual fund, you have to ask yourself, "Did my advisor suggest this because it was the best thing for me, or did he or she do it to make money for him or herself and prevent me from leaving the firm?" And that's a question only you can answer.

Financial Consumer Scorecard

It is how you invest, not what you invest in, that will determine your ultimate success.

How many investment companies, advisors and planners realize protecting your money means protecting your future? How many actually care if you achieve your goals or end up struggling to make ends meet? How many fully appreciate the fundamental importance of protecting your money?

This comparison scorecard is designed for practical people who are interested in evaluating and filtering information to ensure the advice they receive is in their best interest.

This scorecard provides a comparison between what we know is possible and the unfortunate reality many practical investors face. By assessing your current situation we hope this document helps you protect your money and your future.

©2007 Lakes Publishing

	WHAT'S TRULY POSSIBLE	THE UNFORTUNATE REALITY
YOUR EMPOWERMENT AND EDUCATION	Consumer Advocacy - Advice and help that begins with taking your goals into account. They evaluate all of your concerns before recommending any products. Someone who will tell you the truth about the investment industry. They fully disclose the advantages AND disadvantages and ensure you understand both. Access to the fundamental concepts and principles of successful investing. Continually research new techniques & concepts to ensure clients are never left behind.	Advice based on an agenda to sell products and services. Their entire focus is on selling products. Advice based on what is best for the investment advisor. They spend 99% of the time going over advantages and less than 1% going over disadvantages leading to misinformed decisions. Product or service specific advice only. Limited sharing to support an agenda other than their own. Doesn't want to be bothered with research; they are just focused on selling you something.
DILIGENT DISCOVERY	First, your advisors discover if they can actually help you in the long term. If it is discovered that long-term help cannot be provided, you are quickly and efficiently referred to a more appropriate resource.	"Our products and services are right for everyone."
RIGOROUS ANALYSIS	A complete analysis of what you have is completed before any possible solutions are suggested. If it makes sense for you to keep doing what you're doing, you are advised to keep doing it.	There is little or no analysis of your present financial situation. The advisor tries to move as much of your money into their products as possible - regardless of whether it makes sense for you to do it.
SIMPLE AND EASY TO FOLLOW PLAN	The foundation for a plan is created by analysis and an honest appraisal of your strengths and weaknesses. A living plan is created to accommodate your unique situation. It is able to adapt to changing circumstances and achieve milestones.	There is either no plan at all or they provide a preformatted "cookie cutter" plan that is obsolete as soon as it is put on the table. "This is the way it is always done," is used to justify a pace beyond your comfort zone. The plan is fixed. To change it requires starting over. Changes are made to the plan arbitrarily, often based on what is best for the investment advisor - not you.
GUARANTEED PORTFOLIO	Only solutions with guarantees attached are offered. The advisor or institution cares about how much progress your portfolio makes. The quest for performance is less important than ensuring you do not lose what you already have. "The return of my principal is more important than the return on my principal."- Will Rogers	Your hard earned assets are vulnerable. There are many excuses offered for under performing portfolios. Losses are blamed on forces beyond their control. Chasing returns often lead to losing sight of protecting existing assets. See above explanation.
LIVING PLAN	Your investments are continuously monitored to ensure you live to the highest means possible without fear of running out of money.	Your expectations are manipulated. You are told not to spend money when the markets are down or promises of unreasonably high returns are made when the markets are up.

31

Take the Retirement $tress Test
(🐖 The Three Little Pigs Test)

Check the following statements that apply to you to determine how your financial foundation would survive the Big Bad Wolf.

____ I understand how the taxation system and the brokerage and banking industries pertain to me and how I can use these systems to my full advantage.

____ I know that I am paying the least amount of tax legally possible.

____ I feel that every year all available techniques to benefit my situation are fully explained.

____ I spend as much as I want without worry of running out of money.

____ I have clear, written goals and plans to achieve them.

____ I have reviewed all the hybrid investment techniques developed in the last 5 years.

____ I know how much, within $100, I pay in tax as a result of my investments.

____ I understand how the tax law changes of July 2001 (EGTRRA) affect my family. I have utilized it to pass on a significantly higher percentage of my assets to my heirs.

____ I have reviewed all long-term care options (LTC Insurance, Asset Backed Protection, Kennedy-Kassenbaum Plan) and am comfortable with my selection.

____ I'm in control of my financial fate, NOT the other way around. I control my finances, my finances do not control or limit me.

🐺 Score

1-4 House made of straw
5-8 House made of sticks
9-10 House made of bricks

Getting back to the *Consumer Reports* article, the shopper ended the report by saying "In hindsight, I think I would have been better off building my relationship with planners more gradually by having them focus on specific issues such as retirement planning."

What the shopper found out is that if you have college funding issues; go to a college funding specialist. If you are a business owner and you have 401(k) issues, go to a 401(k) specialist.

So if you are retired and need more income or have long-term care issues, go to a retirement specialist who understands the needs of senior investors.

Fifty years ago, there was only one kind of doctor – the kind you went to when you were sick. But today, there are specialists in every type of field you could imagine. Doctors specialize in allergies, skin problems, heart problems, and there are podiatrists, gynecologists, oncologists, even specialized surgeons. So if you have a heart problem, would you go see a doctor who specializes in the human foot? Of course not! You'd go to a heart specialist. So why let an advisor who specializes in college planning (or worse yet, doesn't have a specialty) handle your financial retirement concerns?

DO THE FUN STUFF YOURSELF…AND DELEGATE THE REST!

Of course, there are bound to be some things you can do on your own, and you may find that you are capable of handling certain aspects of your finances by yourself without professional help. If so, that's great.

For example, some people like to take care of their own investments. They enjoy keeping up with their returns, learning about new products they might want to invest in, researching companies, and keeping tabs on Wall Street in general. If you are one of those people, you may want to handle your portfolio yourself rather than hand it over to an advisor.

Other people like to keep track of their expenses and spending. These people love having computer programs that balance their checkbooks, remind them of bills that are due, and help them calculate their taxes. If you are one of those people, you may enjoy handling these things yourself rather than hiring an accountant.

The point is that if you love doing something, then by all means... continue to do it! But if you hate researching stocks and reading the Wall Street Journal, then delegate your portfolio to a capable advisor. Likewise, if you hate dealing with numbers, and the thought of doing your own taxes makes you cringe, then delegate those duties to an accountant.

But there is a catch to doing these things yourself. If you decide to do something like your taxes or your investments yourself, make sure you are just as knowledgeable and capable as a professional. Because if you can't do something as well or as easily as a professional can, it'll be more trouble than it's worth.

For example, when I was in my 20's, I used to change the oil in my car myself and would even give my car tune-ups. I don't do either of those things anymore. Could I if I wanted to? Of course, but it's more convenient for me to pay someone else to maintain my car than to spend a Saturday afternoon doing it myself.

Also, no matter how much you enjoy doing tasks like these, you will need to not only be competent in your abilities, but commit to staying on top of them. Because when you decide to do something like select your own stocks, file your own taxes, or write your own will, you've chosen not to use a professional – and that means you are the professional.

To demonstrate just how important this is, consider your annual tax return. You may be able to fill out a 1040 yourself, but a good accountant keeps up on the new tax laws and can give advice as to how to best reduce taxes, take advantage of tax credits, and avoid things like the alternative minimum tax and an audit. If you're going to take care of your taxes yourself, you need to understand all of these things as well as a professional does. If not, you are better off using an accountant. It may cost more, but you are also getting a lot more for your money.

Likewise, you may be able to buy software that will allow you to draft your own will and handle basic legal matters, but how will you know if something is incorrect or the laws change? Do you want to run the risk of disinheriting members of your family because a computer program gave you incorrect information or didn't notify you of a law change? Of course not. So unless you are an attorney yourself, you'd be wise to spend money on a good lawyer. Because even if you are sure you can do it yourself, there is a high risk in doing so.

The most popular thing people handle on their own is their investments...and that's great! After all, it's your money – you should be keeping tabs on it. During the Internet boom of the 1990's, the mainstream media began referring to investing as the Great American Hobby. And it's no surprise really. Thanks to advances in technology, anyone with a few shares of stock can watch live market activity on CNBC, research stocks online through tools like Morningstar, and even buy and sell their own stocks over the internet. And people who do this on a regular basis are usually very capable of taking care of their own investments. But if you are one of those people, you need to realize that it'll become a big part of your life. Once you commit to handling all your investments on your own, you have to have a constant eye on the market every single day. In today's Wall Street, you can't keep up with your stocks one day and forget about them the next.

So no matter what duties you decide to take on yourself, remember that it's not a hobby. Things like gardening, woodwork, and golf are hobbies. Guarding and securing everything you've earned from 40 years of hard work is not. It's a full-time job that you shouldn't take lightly.

The bottom line is that you need to spend at least three or four hours a week on any task that you decide to handle yourself. So if you enjoy taxes or investing that much, good for you. You'll probably give yourself more attention than a professional would. But if that kind of commitment doesn't sound like fun, don't feel bad. A lot of people are very capable of doing these kinds of tasks, but have decide there are better ways to spend their time.

RESOURCES FOR YOU TO DO IT YOURSELF

Of course, if you decide to take on any of these things yourself, you are going to need resources to help you. While I'm not an expert on taxes or the law, here are some things to assist those of you who plan on handling your own investments:

As we've already mentioned, the Internet is your best tool when it comes to investments. There are a multitude of resources out there for do-it-yourself investors, such as:

- Value Line (http://.www.valueline.com)

- Morningstar (http://www.morningstar.com)

- Motley Fool (http://www.fool.com)

There are also websites that specialize in helping investors with various kinds of investments, as well as subscription websites that provide third-party analysis of stocks and funds. Even the web browsers Google (www.google.com) or Yahoo! have great financial resources (http://finance.yahoo.com). As you can imagine, this is by no means a comprehensive list of web resources, but it should provide you with a good starting point to begin working in this area.

There are also organizations you can join for support and help. One of the most popular is the American Association of Individual Investors, or the AAII (http://www.aaii.com). There is also the National Association of Investors Corporation, or the NAIC (http://www.better-investing.

org). All provide a wealth of information for individual investors of all kinds, as well as a way to network and learn from others. Everyone who handles their own investments should join one such group.

Finally, there are plenty of print resources. You may already be familiar with the Wall Street Journal, but there is also Investor's Business Daily, as well as the Financial Times. And, as you well know, there is an abundance of magazines and books for individual investors – far more than this book could accurately address.

There is one important piece of advice for anyone handling their own investments. As you look for resources that will help you become a better and more knowledgeable investor, make sure you scrutinize everything you read. Not all editorial content is the same, and just because someone wrote it doesn't mean it's true.

So instead of looking for hot stock tips and the "next big thing," focus on information from multiple sources and make up your own mind. You should have at least five sources that you use on a regular basis to ensure that you are getting balanced information. And look for facts and figures, rather than someone telling you what to do. As with anything in life, anyone who tells you what to do has their own agenda and probably doesn't have your best interests at heart.

Those of you who want to do your own taxes should strongly consider J.K. Lasser's books (http://www.jklasser.com). Not only do his books help with filing taxes, but they are full of ideas and suggestions to reduce taxes as well. When it comes to computer software, Turbo Tax is an excellent program.

If you truly want to understand as much as you can about taxes, take the tax classes offered by H&R Block on an annual basis. Information is available on their website (http://www.hrblock.com), and you'll learn most of the same things as their professional tax preparers. However, be sure to take refresher classes every year in order to stay on top of the myriad tax law changes that continuously occur. It's an annual expense that could not only save you money in the long run, but may also give you the opportunity to work as a seasonal tax preparer.

When it comes to online resources, be careful. As with investments, don't assume that everything you read is correct. After all, if there is one organization that you don't want to cross, it's the IRS. You should make sure that any tax reduction strategy you use has been tried and true for many years. Unlike investing, taxes are one aspect of your life where you don't want to be ahead of the pack.

Lastly, there is the prospect of handling your own legal affairs, which is very risky. Unless you are an attorney, the risk of making a mistake or overlooking something is extremely great. In fact, handling your own legal affairs is almost like performing surgery on yourself. Doctors have their own doctors, and even lawyers have their own personal attorneys, so you should consider delegating this one area.

There are lots of websites, books, and software out there that insist they can help you with things like wills and powers of attorney. But the problem is that every situation is different. So while they may provide basic templates for common, ordinary legal forms, the slightest difference from the norm makes them useless. And do you consider your financial situation to be common and ordinary? Just be careful.

CHANGE MY OWN OIL?

So by now you are probably wondering, "Should I even use an advisor, or should I just do it myself?" Well, there is no easy answer. And the truth is that it depends on what you are trying to accomplish.

Unfortunately, no one can answer that question for you. But before you decide to go it alone, spend some time and assess your current situation. Take a step back and take a long, hard look at the big picture. For example you may need to analyze your annual income:

- Do you expect it to go up or down in the future?

- How much can you safely pull out each year?

- What is your chance of running out of money if the market tanks?

- How will your financial situation change if your spouse were to die?

- How will your financial situation change for your spouse if you were to die?

You also need to determine how long you and your spouse are likely to live. Is there a chance you'll run out of money? How much can you afford to spend annually? How much money do you need each month to maintain your current standard of living?

Cash flow is another area that you need to review. What are your expenses likely to be in the future? What kinds of things might change or interrupt your cash flow?

You also need to consider possible events that may impact your life:

- Is long-term care a possibility for you or your spouse?

- Is your home paid for?

- What would happen if you needed to move?

- What would happen if your children or grandchildren ever needed a significant sum of money?

The last thing you will need to consider is your legal and financial paperwork, because having the right things in place won't do much good if you forget a few key pieces of documentation.

- Does all your legal and financial paperwork list the correct beneficiaries?

- If you became incapacitated, would your spouse be able to handle your investments?

- What would happen to your investments if both you and your spouse were to die?

- Are you sure your investments will go to your children, or will Uncle Sam and the taxman get their hands on the American Dream you've built for yourself?

- Will your investments and years of hard work be lost to probate costs or attorney fees?

As you can see, there are a lot of questions you need to ask yourself, and you'll need to have thorough and complete answers to them. A guess or an estimate won't cut it. And as you might expect, it takes time to answer these questions thoroughly, not to mention the ongoing time commitment needed to stay on top of current information and changes in these areas. Again, are you willing to spend hours every week doing the necessary research on tax laws benefiting trusts, researching investments, and implementing the proper planning?

Sit down and ask yourself these questions, along with any others you think are important to you and your family's financial health. Once you do that you'll truly know where you stand. And then you can set your goals.

Maybe you are planning on leaving as much of your money as possible to your children and grandchildren. Maybe you want to have a lifestyle of luxury and travel as a reward for all your years of hard work. Or maybe you simply want to live comfortably without ever worrying that you will run out of money. No matter what the answer, you now have your financial goal. Once you've answered these questions, you'll have a created a roadmap that will guide you throughout the rest of financial life.

HOW TO CHOOSE ADVISORS FOR DELEGATED TASKS

We've already discussed some of the traits that you should expect from a financial advisor and how to tell if you need a new one. But what should you do if it's time to find a financial professional who cares more about your needs than lining their own pockets?

The most important thing you can do is look for someone who specializes in your needs and goals. Having already done the legwork of evaluating your current financial situation, you already know what you need to accomplish, so it's time to find someone who can fulfill those goals.

Yet finding a true specialist is easier said than done. For example, if you're looking to minimize your taxes on your investments, just about every advisor you speak to will insist that they can help you. And while they may have a product or two up their sleeve that they insist is tax-free, you'll have to do some legwork to evaluate them on your own. But don't worry; we'll get to that in a minute.

This applies to any financial professional you hire, be it an accountant, attorney, advisor, or insurance agent. If you are looking for someone to do your taxes, make sure that the person you hire does taxes for a lot of people just like you – in other words, is familiar with retired individuals who hold significant investments. Likewise, business owners should find an accountant who specializes in taxes for small businesses. And if you have one professional who truly specializes in your needs, ask him or her for a referral. Odds are that your accountant may know an insurance agent who specializes in long-term health care, or your financial advisor may know an attorney who regularly handles wills and estates for retired individuals.

When it comes to taxes, many people wonder if they need a Certified Public Accountant or if a tax preparer is enough. The truth is that a CPA is seldom necessary, unless you have a complicated situation. For example, if you've sold a significant amount of property or investments and are concerned about capital gains, an accountant might be worth the additional fee.

However, even individuals who file their own taxes should have a tax professional review their taxes every three years, regardless of their situation. Having your returns reviewed will likely cost less than paying to have them done. But by getting them reviewed, you will not only have made sure that everything is correct, but you may learn about a new law or tax change that affects you.

When it comes to selecting a property casualty insurance agent, you should be diligent in interviewing potential agents. Ask them how they intend to make sure you are paying the least amount in premiums every year, as well as how they plan to make sure you are always fully covered. Good agents have systems in place to keep up-to-date on their clients' needs.

You should consider an independent agent, because like an independent advisor, they are able to shop around with several companies for the best deal possible. You can certainly interview captive agents, but you'll need to be skeptical. That's because a captive agent who works for one particular company, only sells that company's products. And of course, if they can only sell one company's policies, they are obviously going to insist that theirs is the best. That doesn't mean you shouldn't buy insurance from a captive agent, but it does mean that before you do, you had better be certain it's the best policy for you.

And thanks to the Internet, you can now even save money by cutting out the middleman. Companies like Geico (http://www. geico. com) and USAA (http://www.usaa.com) allow individuals to shop around on their own and buy their own insurance. While this can save money, the downside is that you don't have a local agent to help you when problems and accidents arise.

Personally, I prefer having an individual in town that I can go to that I know will stand up for me if I need assistance with a difficult claim. I'm in no way suggesting that non-agent companies such as Geico and USAA aren't high quality, reputable companies. I just feel better looking a real human being in the eye, shaking their hand, and knowing that when they tell me I'm covered, I am.

Like any other professional, you should expect your agent to meet with you on an annual basis and review your current policy to make sure it's adequate. For example, people's homes often appreciate in value, yet they forget to increase their homeowner's policy to reflect that increase. When that happens and damage occurs to the house, the homeowner may pay a significant amount of the repairs out of pocket because of this oversight. Of course, this kind of personalized service may cost a bit more, but you are paying for a higher level of service.

HOW TO PICK A GOOD FINANCIAL ADVISOR

So what do you do if it's time for a change? Well, if you've decided to fire your current financial advisor and you begin looking for someone new, here are a few things that can help you along the way:

1) Get information from the SEC if you are working with a stockbroker

Obviously, you want to have not only a reputable advisor, but one who works for a firm you can trust. The U.S. Securities and Exchange Commission (SEC) protects investors and maintains the integrity of the securities markets. They help investors like you by enforcing federal and state securities laws which require advisors and their firms to be licensed or registered. The SEC also requires that information about any disciplinary action be made public.

The SEC website has investor information with tips on everything from making complaints, to explanations of investments, to calculators that help with social security and retirement planning. It's available on the web at http://www.sec.gov.

Even though the SEC requires information about advisors and firms be made available to the public, they do not provide that information themselves.

This information is available through the Central Registration Depository (CRD). The CRD is a computer database that contains information about brokers and firms, and it can provide a wealth of information that can help you make the right decision. The CRD will tell you if an advisor is licensed to sell investments in your state, if they have been disciplined by the SEC, and if other investors have filed complaints about the advisor. You will also learn about the advisor's educational background and other firms he or she has worked for in the past.

2) Check out your broker

As an investor, you can't access the CRD yourself. But there are two ways you can get this information. You can either contact your state securities regulator, or ask the Financial Industry Regulators Authority (FINRA) to give you this information.

The best way to find your state securities regulator is through the North American Securities Administrators Association. Their website is http://www.nasaa.org. Or you can call them at the number provided on their website. They can provide contact information for your state's securities regulator, who can look up advisors for you.

You can also ask FINRA to check out a broker or firm for you. They accept requests through both the Internet and over the phone and are often the fastest and easiest way to get this information. Learn more on the FINRA website at http://www.FINRA.org, or call them at the number listed on their website.

3) Find out if your broker is certified

There are several certifications available to advisors. In order to find a good advisor, you should look for and understand some of the more important certifications for your needs.

4) Check out organizations your broker is affiliated with

Many organizations are specifically designed to help educate and protect seniors during their retirement years. Be sure to check out your broker's affiliations to ensure they have your best interest at heart.

Once you've found the right advisor, you should ask some questions during your first meeting with him or her. Remember that although you want a good advisor, he or she also wants your business. So don't be afraid to treat a meeting with a potential advisor as an interview.

Now that you've determined just what it is you are trying to accomplish and have selected the best advisors and professionals for your needs, let's get into the nitty-gritty of senior planning. In the next chapter we'll discuss tax planning as one of the best ways to keep the money you've earned.

CHAPTER 5

TAX PLANNING

"There is nothing sinister in so arranging one's affairs so as to make taxes as low as possible."

"Everybody does so, rich or poor, and do right, for nobody owes any public duty to pay more taxes than the law demands."

"Taxes are enforced exactions, not voluntary contributions."

JUSTICE LEARNED HAND
UNITED STATES APPELLATE COURT

WHEN IT COMES TO PROTECTING your piece of the American Dream, the biggest problem all of us face is taxes. We all know that the tax man wants as much money as he can get, and year after year he just keeps on taking from taxpayers. Even worse, if you manage to make more money, the tax man expects you to give him even more of it.

It seems that every time we come into contact with money, we are taxed. We pay taxes when we earn it, we pay taxes when we spend it, we pay taxes when we save it, we pay taxes when we give it to someone else, and we are going to pay taxes when we die. Yet what's funny is that our country was founded by people who were tired of paying so many taxes!

A BRIEF HISTORY OF THE TAX CODE

Think about the Boston Tea Party; all that tea was dumped into the Boston harbor because Americans were letting England know that they weren't going to pay taxes on their tea. Our forefathers took a stand against taxation without representation, but look at where we are in the 21st century. Do you believe you are being well represented when it comes to taxes? Did you vote to have your Social Security income taxed? How about the taxes that are added to your cell phone bill? Most people pay a city and state tax just for using a cell phone. You certainly didn't ask for that. Your city and state simply added them on because they decided it was for a good cause.

Until recently, our country had a $3 trillion surplus. Of course, once the economy stumbled and we began the war in Iraq after September 11, 2001, that amount quickly disappeared. Now we have a deficit, and some people insist that our taxes are needed to fight the war on terrorism and keep America going. But is that actually true?

In the late 1990's when we supposedly had a surplus, I began asking people if they believed that our country's surplus really existed. The vast majority said "no", and many thought it was an outright lie.

Two things had to happen in order for that surplus to last. First, we were told that the surplus would last if we did not have a recession in the next 10 years. Of course, the late 90's was a time when the United States was in the longest economic expansion period of its history. So spending was increasing almost daily. Regardless, everyone will agree that the economy took a tumble after September 11, 2001. And while things bounced back, the recovery was temporary. We are still trying to recover from the Great Recession of 2008!

Second, we were told that in order for the surplus to last the United States would have to cut its spending by 20% over the same 10 years. Our country has never had a president who left office spending less than when he took office. Many have pointed out that President Reagan spent less during his term in office. But once debt issuances were included, this was no longer the case. Most importantly, Congress didn't even include the biggest debt this country has, Social Security, in its supposed surplus.

An article from CBS *Market Watch* in October 2003 summed up the state of things. At the time, the projected budget deficit for fiscal year 2004 was $600 billion, thanks in part to the war in Iraq. Yet as President Bush's term in office continued, we saw unlimited tax cuts for the ultra-wealthy and limitless spending. And as we are all aware, the deficit exploded during President Obama's first term as President. By the time our soldiers leave Iraq, who knows what the final tally will be.

According to William Gale, an economist with the senior Bush's Council of Economic Advisors, and Peter Orszag, a special assistant to Clinton on economic policy, our nation had gone from an annual surplus of $127 billion in 2001 to a $300 billion deficit in 2003. These PhD-educated economists also expected the deficit to double in2004 and determined that the overall federal account would shift from a long-term surplus of $5.6 trillion to a deficit of $2.3 trillion.

What's worse, according to Gale and Orszag, was that the official numbers used by the government were misleading because they were based on accounting measures that would have made Enron green with envy.

First, the government bases its figures on the assumption that sunset provisions tied to temporary taxes will never occur. In other words, the government expects that current "temporary" taxes will eventually become permanent.

Second, the government assumes that federal spending will only go up with inflation and not outpace it. As we've seen over the last few years, that's hardly the case.

Lastly, the government is able to make the deficit appear lower because cash flow surpluses from Social Security, Medicare, and federal employee pensions are not included in their accounting methods.

Now, imagine what will happen when baby boomers continue to retire in the next 10 years. This potential drain on Medicare and Social Security hasn't even been taken into account.

In order to balance the budget, Gale and Orszag insist that Social Security and Medicare spending would have to be cut by 41%. Of course, no politician is ever going to vote for that kind of a cut for Social Security and Medicare, but does that mean you shouldn't worry? Not hardly.

The bottom line is a real surplus never existed, and today we have a huge deficit. That means that we all have to pay taxes to fund our military, education, welfare and the rest.

Our spending has dramatically increased over the last several years... and that spending threatens to increase our taxes.

Congress claims to have enacted lots of tax law changes over the last few years to help us all out. But has it made a difference?

All the restructuring that's gone on the past few years is really nothing but congressional tax shenanigans. As usual, the wealthy pay less in taxes. And who is asked to pick up the slack? Middle income America (the backbone of this country).

But remember the analogy about playing by the rules? As investors, your response to these shenanigans should be to develop a tax strategy that takes advantage of the rules and arranges your affairs accordingly.

When it comes to taxes, this is what you should strive to do. In fact, it is possible for many senior investors to pay only 4% in taxes on their income by using just a few techniques. It may sound too good to be true, but everything we will discuss in this chapter is absolutely legal. This is not about offshore trusts or tax-dodging schemes, but applying 30-year-old tax strategies to your investments – most likely, things that no one has ever gone over with you.

Take another look at the quote in the beginning of this chapter. Judge Hand basically said that as U.S. citizens we are allowed to arrange our affairs in order to pay the least amount in taxes legally possible. In fact, he said it is our duty to do so. After all, isn't that what our country was founded on?

I'm proud to be an American and willing to pay my fair share of taxes, as long as our government gives me something in return such as improved roads, better schools, and military defense. But our government also wastes an awful lot of money...money it also gets from hard-working Americans like you and me. And you and I can be just as proud of America for half as much money. Don't you agree?

The New York Tycoon

There was once a very wealthy New York tycoon who needed to borrow $10,000 for a trip to Europe. When he went to his bank to borrow the money, the young banker asked the tycoon what he intended to use as collateral for the loan.

"My Rolls Royce is parked outside," he told the young banker. "You're welcome to hold it until I pay you back."

The banker agreed that the car would suffice, so he took the tycoon's keys and placed the Rolls Royce in a secured garage to protect it from damage and theft. Once it was securely parked, the banker finished the loan, and the tycoon left with his $10,000.

Two weeks later, the tycoon returned from his trip and went to the bank. "I've come back to pay off my loan and get my car back," he told the young banker.

"Of course," the banker responded. As the two were finishing up the loan paperwork, the banker had the Rolls Royce brought from the secure garage. "I must admit that I'm confused," he told the tycoon. "When filling out the paperwork for the loan, I did a credit check on you and found out that you're worth more than $30 million. With so much money, why did you need to borrow $10,000?"

"Where else in Manhattan can you park your car in a secure garage for $37 a week," the tycoon laughed. The tycoon wasn't breaking the rules by borrowing money to park his car; instead, he was using them to his advantage. He's a perfect example of someone who knows the rulebook and uses it in his favor.

A TAX ON A TAX

While there are some taxes you can't do anything about, there are four taxes that you can significantly reduce with a little bit of easy planning!

1. You can reduce taxes on your interest and dividends

2. You can reduce taxes on your capital gains

3. You can reduce or eliminate taxes on your death

4. Many investors can reduce or eliminate taxes on Social Security income.

Social Security is one of the most important areas to address when looking at your tax situation. Taxes on your Social Security income are a tax on a tax. Social Security was a tax you were forced to pay for all of those working years, and now you are still taxed when you get that money back. The government gets you coming and going!

Several times a year, I attend symposiums for the financial services industry. And at these gatherings, I ask my fellow associates what they are doing about their clients' Social Security tax.

"Nothing," they always tell me. "It's no big deal." Of course, they say that because it's not a big deal to them. But 20 or 30 years from now when they start drawing Social Security, they'll have a different view. And any advisor who thinks this way does not have your best interests at heart.

As you know, FDR created Social Security back in 1935. And three years later people started receiving benefits. At the time, the U.S. Treasury said that Social Security was a gift and that it would never be taxed. Well, to be honest, it wasn't a gift. Since when do you have to pay for a gift?

But even though FDR promised that Social Security would never be taxed, look at what happened. It shouldn't be surprising; after all, what do politicians find easy to make, but hard to keep? Promises.

Unlike most politicians, FDR kept his promise. But in 1983, Congress created a law that allowed 50% of your Social Security income to be taxed. To make matters worse, Congress increased that amount to 85% in 1993. And it won't be long before Congress decides it's okay to tax that last 15%.

When you worked, did you and your fellow employees meet in a back room once a year to vote yourselves raises? That's what Congress does. Every year, members of Congress meet. And despite current layoffs, a bad job market, and people with little money to spend, Congress gives itself an increase in salary. It usually happens on a Saturday night, so that it attracts little attention in the Sunday newspaper...and by Monday, other news has made people forget all about it.

Factor in that most members of Congress are either millionaires or owe their election to gifts from millionaires, and they have little incentive to lower taxes on Social Security income. Since it doesn't affect them, why should they care?

- 66% of Senators are Millionaires
- 41% of the House of Representatives are Millionaires
- 1% of Americans are Millionaires

*Though in 2011 Congress finally got the message and voted to block the annual pay raise.[2]

WHEN IS "TAX FREE" NOT TAX FREE?

If you own tax-free municipal bonds, you may already realize that they aren't really tax-free. When you file your 1040 every year, you have to report any tax free interest you receive, which includes interest from these bonds. So if these bonds are truly tax-free, why are you required to report the interest?

Because they are taxed when you begin receiving Social Security.

Tax-free municipal bonds are tax-free for people in their 20's, 30's, 40's, and 50's. But for retirees? No way. You are taxed when you draw Social Security. Washington continues to treat the Greatest Generation poorly...and that's a crime.

I once met a woman who exemplified this perfectly. As she introduced herself, she was feeling very proud because her broker had put her in $250,000 worth of municipal bonds. The woman took out her statement and showed me. I looked at the statement and said, "Oh, I'm so sorry."

"What do you mean?" she said.

I asked if I could see her tax return. When she showed it to me, I immediately saw that those $250,000 of municipal bonds were causing her to pay an additional $3,000 in taxes each year.

Talk about killing the messenger! Once I explained this to her, I was barely able to get her out of the office while I was still alive. Apparently, the truth can hurt.

It was obvious that her broker had never looked at the woman's tax return. So do you think her broker ever explained to her that her tax-exempt bonds could be taxable? Absolutely not.

This can be confusing if you don't understand how Social Security is taxed. So if you want to know just how much of your Social Security is being taxed, get your most recent 1040 and do the following:

1. Add lines 7 and 8a

2. Add line 8b (tax-free income)

3. Add lines 9 through 19

4. If you are married and earn more than $32,000 (or single and earn more than $25,000) add 50% of your Social Security Income.

   If you are married and earn more than $44,000 (or single and earn more than $34,000) add 85% of your Social Security income.

This total is your provisional income, and the IRS uses this number to determine how much of your Social Security income is taxed. You can see that the tax on your Social Security is based on a lot more than just your Social Security income.

THE GOOD STEWARD IS PUNISHED

Do you see how the system is designed to work against you? It's frustrating because not only did your generation build this county, but you were also good savers. You believed that "a penny saved is a penny earned" and trusted the motto "waste not, want not." Your taxes made Social Security what it is today; yet instead of being thanked and rewarded for your efforts, you are being taxed. Quite simply, you are a generation of good stewards who are being punished for your hard work.

On top of this, each year the tax brackets go up a little bit so that they are adjusted for inflation. This means the income needed to reach the 15% tax bracket goes up a little bit, the income needed to reach the

28% tax bracket goes up a little bit, and so does the income needed to reach all of the other brackets.

Your deductions are also indexed for inflation. So are your exemptions. In fact, everything is indexed for inflation **except for... you guessed it, Social Security.** This means that since the IRS started taxing Social Security in 1983, they have not indexed any of those Social Security brackets for inflation.

Of course, in 1983, $32,000 was a pretty darn good income. At the time:

- The average income was $21,073 a year

- The average home cost $82,600

- The average car cost $8,577.

That was 20 years ago. What is $32,000 going to get you today? Not much.

So when Congress and politicians tell you that they are going to help you reduce your taxes, you should be skeptical. After all, how much have the recent tax breaks helped you? Probably not much.

THE BOTTOM LINE

What is really upsetting is that seniors are the most influential group of voters in this country. AARP has more clout on Capitol Hill than anyone else, and no politician in their right mind would speak out against AARP. But we still get hoodwinked by having our Social Security subject to double taxation.

The bottom line is that it's the same as it's always been. The people who benefit the most from the recent tax law changes are the very wealthy. The vast majority of middle-class, hardworking people like you will not benefit from these tax law changes.

So, how do you get a tax break? You become informed.

HOW YOUR INVESTMENTS ARE TAXED

Now that we've talked about municipal bonds being taxed and the importance of reducing your taxes on your Social Security, we are going to discuss mutual funds. And when it comes to mutual funds, there are a few key things you need to know.

First, you should understand that all mutual funds must distribute 90% of everything they earn as capital gains and dividends. If you've owned a mutual fund for more than a year, you'll receive a tax form 1099 as a result. This reflects your capital gains and dividends, which means even though you are holding the fund, you still have to pay taxes on it.

Of course, we were all told how much the new tax treatment of dividends was going to help us. Just about everyone in Washington explained time and again that we'd get a huge boon from this change. But in hindsight, who did it really help?

The tax-favored status of dividends is wonderful for the super-rich. All of their shares of DuPont, Exxon, or whatever company from which they receive dividends puts them in the tax bracket of a waitress. On the other hand, the middle-class, which owns mutual funds (instead of millions of dollars in individual company stock) are once again taken to the cleaners. This is because mutual funds pay the internal fees using dividends first. That means the tax-favored status of dividends is gobbled up by fund fees. As a result, you won't ever receive the tax advantage from this status.

THIS RATIO KILLS RETURNS

Depending on your experience with mutual funds, you may or may not know what a "turnover ratio" is. Turnover ratio is a statistical way of saying how many stocks are bought and sold by a mutual fund each year. For example, let's say you own a mutual fund that invests in 100 different stocks, and that fund has an annual turnover ratio of 94%. This means that out of those 100 stocks, the fund manager is going to sell 94 of them this year, and replace each of those with a different stock.

By today's standards, a turnover ratio of 130%[3] is considered average. Yet 10 years ago, the average turnover ratio was only 24%. Each year this ratio has gone up, and some fund managers are selling and buying stocks as if they were day traders. I've seen mutual funds with a 400% turnover ratio. This means that if the fund has 100 stocks, the fund manager will sell all 100 stocks, and then replace them with something different. And he's going to do it again, and again, and again. In other words, he's going to sell every stock in the fund an average of four times over the course of just one year. Each stock in the fund would be held for an average of just three months.

And if you own a mutual fund with a high turnover ratio, you can imagine what it would do to your tax situation. Every time the manager sold a stock, he or she would have capital gains to contend with. And we said a moment ago, 90% of all capital gains must be distributed – which means they give them to you, and you end up paying taxes on them.

Of course in theory, fund managers who buy and sell stocks on a constant basis do so to improve the fund's returns and capital gains, but it rarely turns out that way. Their hearts are in the right place –but you get clobbered when it comes to taxes.

Look at it this way: when you sell a stock within 12 months of buying it, the stock is considered short-term. And when you sell a stock more than 12 months after buying it, the stock is considered long-term.

As you know, short-term gains are much worse for taxes than long-term gains. In fact, short-term gains mean you'll pay anywhere from 33% to 50% more in taxes than you would for long-term gains.

So if a manager is constantly buying and selling stocks inside a mutual fund, the tax treatment of that fund is going to be extremely poor. But your advisor is probably not telling you that.

FE FIFO HIFO FUM

Another issue that affects taxes of mutual funds is, "which shares are sold and when"? Anyone that calculates capital gains on their taxes is familiar with the different kinds of record keeping the IRS will accept. There is FIFO (First In, First Out) which is the most expensive way of handling capital gains, and there is HIFO (Highest In, First Out) which means that they are selling the highest-priced shares of that company first, regardless of when you purchased them.

Let's say you've bought some shares of XYZ stock at $10, some more at $20, and some more at $30. Now you want to sell some of those shares, and the going price is $40 a share. You would want to sell the shares using HIFO, which would give you a minimal gain of $10 on each share. If you sold the same number of shares using FIFO, you'd see a gain of $30 per share, and you'd pay more in taxes... even though you'd receive the same amount for your sale. That's a huge difference!

Most people who don't know better (or haven't kept good records) determine their gains by using the FIFO method. But as you can see, those who take the time to keep track of their transactions often use the HIFO method and save themselves a lot of money on capital gains taxes in the process. The IRS doesn't care which method you use, as long as you are consistent and your records support the method you choose.

Well, mutual fund managers are just like individual investors when it comes to their capital gains. Some go to the trouble of keeping good records and using the HIFO method to save money on capital gains, while other funds don't worry about it and are forced to use the FIFO method. About an equal number of funds use each method, meaning there is a 50/50 split between users of FIFO and HIFO.

Mutual Fund magazine once asked funds that use FIFO why they didn't use the HIFO method since it would save their investors' money on capital gains. The majority of fund companies replied that it was just too much work to keep track of it that way.

It's easy to say something is too much work when someone else has to deal with the repercussions of your laziness. So while funds may not think it's important to bother with using HIFO, you'll pay the price for their laziness – in extra taxes. Warning: It gets even worse because of a recent tax law change. Individual stocks and bonds in your Brokerage Account will fall prey to this very same problem beginning in 2013.

PHANTOM INCOME

By far, one of the most frustrating things about mutual funds is "phantom income". This occurs when you lose money on a mutual fund, but still get hit with a HUGE tax bill at the end of the year. A few years ago when every fund was making money this was almost unheard of. But today, it's becoming a common occurrence. If you want to avoid phantom income, watch your fund's capital gains and turnover ratio.

Even if you ignore the tax issues, high turnover rates are still a bad thing. Let's say that a fund manager sells off $30 million of a particular stock in his fund. When he or she sells that much stock, the price of the stock usually goes down in response to selling pressure. So at this point, the manager may end up with $29 million in cash from the process of the sale (remember selling pressure caused the price to drop as he sold). Now let's say the manager uses that cash to purchase a new stock. And when someone purchases that much stock of one company, the price of the stock goes up due to buying pressure. So at this point, the fund now has $28 million of the new company's stock.

In other words, the fund started out with $30 million of the old stock, and replaced it with $28 million of another stock (because of the buying and selling pressure affecting the price). When this happens, the fund has to recoup two million dollars just to break even. That means the fund manager now has to take more risk in the market to cover his loss. Essentially, the higher the turnover ratio, the riskier the fund.

GOOD FOR THE GOOSE…BUT NOT THE GANDER?

By the way, isn't it interesting that advisors tell us to buy and hold stocks, then turn right around and suggest funds where the managers are churning through stocks on an almost daily basis? It's as if what's good for the goose isn't good for the gander. So if you are a buy-and-hold investor, you owe it to yourself to make sure your funds are buy-and-hold as well. And the best way to find this out is by comparing turnover ratios.

The bottom line is that you should take the time to learn about your funds and understand that not all funds are created equal. CNNfn says that one of the darkest secrets of the mutual fund industry is that taxes can wipe out a significant chunk of your investment returns. Neil Wolfson, a tax expert with the accounting firm KPMG, says most investors have been in the dark about mutual funds. He believes the majority of investors remain woefully uniformed about the tax implications of a fund manager's trading decisions. And not surprisingly, Joel

Dickson, a Vanguard Group principal, says that while there are thousands of funds, only 30 or so are tax-managed. So if your fund has a high turnover ratio, you could be writing a big check to Uncle Sam.

It's very easy to determine or find the turnover ratio of a fund. If your advisor can't do that for you, you should ask yourself whether he or she is looking out for you or themselves.

Above all, make sure you know not just the fund's rate of return, but your rate of return net of taxes. What matters is not how much money the fund makes, but how much money you get to keep.

STOP PAYING TAXES ON MONEY YOU'RE NOT SPENDING

The most important thing you can do is stop paying taxes on money you aren't spending. Of course, if you are spending your money, good for you. You've worked hard for it, so spend it and enjoy yourself. But if you aren't spending your money, don't pay taxes on it.

The best way to do this is by positioning your money in investments where taxes are handled on a deferred basis. Some investors disagree, and you might be rolling your eyes right now.

"That's a problem waiting to happen," is a common response. "I'm going to have to pay taxes on it eventually, so why not just pay now?"

Because paying now is actually more costly than deferring your taxes!

Let's say that you have a tax bill of $2,000 per year, but you've decided to defer it for 10 years. So you defer $2,000 in year one and another $2,000 in year two, and you continue to do this for 10 years. Now during this time, you continue to grow that money at 6% in a bank, stock, bond, etc. At the end of those 10 years, your deferred tax has grown to $36,000 thanks to your investments.

Of course, you still have to pay taxes on the money. You have to pay the $20,000 you deferred ($2,000 per year x 10 years). And you will have to pay tax on the $16,000 gain. Uncle Sam could conceivably take up to one-third of your $16,000 (assuming you are in the highest tax bracket). That would take $5,330 but leave you with $10,670 after tax...just by deferring!

Compare this to your grumpy old friend who said you were being a fool. He was in the same situation and decided to pay his taxes each year. He pays $2,000 in the first year, another $2,000 in the second year, and so on for the next 10 years. Once everything is done, your friend has paid $20,000 in taxes over the course of those 10 years...and he doesn't keep anything.

No one in their right mind wants to end up with nothing when they can end up with $10,670. So don't pay taxes on money you aren't spending.

We would all like more income and fewer taxes, and you can **have your cake and eat it too** if you take advantage of two provisions in the tax code.

IRS Reg 1.72-2(b) and IRS code section 72(b)(1) can help. These enable you to take advantage of exclusion ratios and can be used to create a split tax plan that will reduce taxes on your income. The exclusion ratio idea is contrary to the old idea of "spend your interest to save your principal." We've all had that ingrained in us. But in order to take advantage of these provisions, you'll have to think differently.

These provisions provide a way to arrange your affairs so that you pay 1.5% tax on your income instead of paying up to 33% in tax. They allow you to increase your income while reducing your taxes and may cut your taxes on capital gains in half. You probably aren't familiar with this, but don't you think you should be?

UNDERSTANDING TAXES AS IT PERTAINS TO THE RETIRED PERSON

In order to understand how taxes are affecting you, it's necessary to look at your annual tax return in light of your investments. So while your accountant may handle your tax return and your advisor may handle your portfolio, these documents need to be compared to each other.

The first step is for you and your advisor to go through your tax return every year. I said your Financial Advisor should review your return with you...NOT just your Accountant. A good Financial Advisor will save you far more on taxes then your accountant can. Schedule an appointment, and sit down with him or her to review your 1040. If your advisor is on the ball, there are several areas he or she may be able to help you with.

Begin by looking at lines 8a and 8b. You will probably find income you could defer. For example, do you have income from municipal bonds? If so, it could be causing you to pay increased taxes on your Social Security. Also, look at line 9 for help with sheltering dividends. Look at line 12 if you own your own business and line 13 for help in reducing capital gains. Line 16 will help with your exclusion ratio, and line 20b will tell you how much of your Social Security is being taxed.

If you are reinvesting interest from savings bonds, annuities or the cash value on your life insurance, you won't pay federal, state or Social Security tax.

The point is that you need to fully explore all your choices for reinvested taxable money. You should not pay taxes on money that is growing and that you aren't spending.

Of course, if you are comfortable with how much you are paying in taxes each April, don't worry about it. Some people such as Ross Perot put all of their money in municipal bonds and don't worry about taxes on social security. But the rest of us (who aren't rich) could use some help.

Tax Deferral and Annuities

Although there are a variety of tools to defer taxes, annuities are the most popular way to do

> Most municipal bonds aren't taxed for federal purposes, but they can be taxed for social security purposes, depending on your income. Federal bonds, on the other hand, are taxed for federal purposes and Social Security, but not for state purposes.

so. But not all annuities are good, and you need to be cautious of insurance companies and agents when considering these products.

Many annuity companies lure investors with a high interest rate for the first year, but lower it to sub-par levels once the interest rate renews in the second year. Like many senior investors, you may have realized this too late. Many of you opened up annuities years ago and are no longer happy with your current interest rates. You realize that other companies pay higher interest rates, but you are rightly concerned that if you move your money, you'll have to pay taxes.

But if you are in this situation, there is good news; IRS code section 1035 allows you to refinance old annuities so you can get a higher interest rate. This section allows you to move your annuity to a new company without having to pay any taxes.

Another concern is penalties. Some companies require investors to pay a surrender penalty if they transfer their money to a different annuity. Fortunately, there are a handful of companies with high interest rates that will pay your surrender penalty for you.

So if your annuity is low interest, you owe it to yourself to shop around for a better interest rate and to refinance the annuity when you find one. If you are currently receiving a low interest rate from your annuity and you don't shop, you are letting your insurance company take a higher profit off your investment. And most of us aren't so generous as to give large corporations an extra bit of our money.

Although we've discussed the benefits of tax-deferral, there is something even better – paying no tax at all! What if your insurance company agreed to pay the taxes for you upon your death? It would certainly save your children and spouse a lot of headache, not to mention money. Some annuity companies realize this, and there are a handful of companies that pay an extra 28% on your gains to cover the taxes associated with them.

"I'm Spending My Kids' Inheritance!"

Many senior investors say, "We've done a good job providing for our kids. We sent them to a good college and gave them good values...so they're entitled to whatever is left over after taxes....but only after we're done with it ourselves!" There isn't anything wrong with that, but if you are concerned about the amount of taxes your children will pay once you are gone, just be mindful that there are companies out there that will pay them. You just need to find those companies and start investing with them.

NOT ALL ANNUITIES ARE GOOD

But before you start moving your money around, remember this: not all annuities are good. In fact, brokers often put variable annuities inside an IRA, something you should generally avoid at all costs. FINRA is the regulatory agency that issues and revokes licenses. They also fine dealers who break the rules. In 1999 FINRA put out a Notice (# 99-35) stating that a variable annuity inside of an IRA is almost never a good thing. The notice also stressed that the person who puts money into these kinds of investments should have an extremely strong and compelling reason for doing so.

So if a variable annuity is inside your IRA, ask your advisor why. If they can't give you a really good reason for this, you are flushing 5% to 20% of your annual return down the toilet. Just as you were with low interest rate annuities, you are simply giving away more of your hard-earned money.

Another major problem with variable annuities is the Income Benefit Riders. These promise the investor a supposed 6% or 7% guaranteed interest rate. The problem with these riders is that they are very complex. Make sure you read all the fine print or you may be in for a nasty surprise. And please, NEVER take your advisor's word for how it works. Have them show it to you in writing!

ARE B SHARES OKAY TO OWN IN A MUTUAL FUND?

Class B shares are another problem inside mutual funds. This has become a fairly regular problem, and many people say they bought Class B shares because they were "no-load" as long as they stayed in the fund for six or seven years.

Unfortunately, that's not true. B shares are loaded with 12(b)-1 fees. These 12(b)-1 fees are disclosed inside the prospectus for B shares, but most investors overlook it or don't read the prospectus at all. So if your mutual fund has B shares, look at the prospectus. And if you're paying 12(b)-1 fees in your mutual fund, you are probably being overcharged roughly 1% a year for the six or seven years the B shares are in the fund.

Let's say that you have $85,000 in your IRA, and your spouse has $55,000 in his or her IRA. The two of you have well over $100,000 combined in your IRAs.

And if both of the IRA's have B shares, you are paying a lot of money for that privilege; it's just more money you are giving away. Why? Because owning B shares is like buying an egg from a farmer for $0.25, then coming back a week later to buy 1,000 eggs. If you return to buy that many eggs, you must really like them. Well, the farmer will appreciate the fact that you are willing to buy so many eggs at one time, so he'll probably give you a break on the price. More than likely, you'd end up paying much less than $0.25 for each egg because of the volume you are buying.

Mutual funds work the same way. Companies have to give you break points and lower your initial sales costs if you invest a certain amount of money in the fund.

Most of the time, advisors put investors into B shares rather than A shares because it means more money for the advisor. This has become such a big problem that the Securities and Exchange Commission (SEC) has said that every salesperson should disclose and keep records of available break points.

Yet the vast majority of people who own B shares do not know about break-points. If an advisor recommends B shares over A shares, but does not give any proof of how this benefits the customer, disciplinary action could be taken against the advisor. So be aware of variable annuities inside of your IRA, as well as B shares inside your mutual fund.

WHAT TO DO WITH ALL THAT IRA AND 401(K) MONEY

Thirty years ago, the biggest asset most people in the United States owned was their house. Today, it's their IRA. And like most retired investors, you've probably accumulated quite a bit of money in your IRA. It's a great deal, but once you start pulling money out of it, you have to pay taxes on it. Of course, we'd all like to take money out of our IRA without paying taxes on it. The problem is that just isn't possible. But many people aren't aware that you can take your money out in a tax-efficient manner.

Would you also like to increase the value of your IRA by 300% or more? Obviously we'd all like to do that! The catch is that this isn't for you, but your beneficiaries – it benefits your kids and grandkids.

There is a provision in the tax code that allows you to defer taxation of your IRA for up to two generations.

Let's say that at your death your spouse inherits your IRA and defers the taxes over his or her lifetime. But once your spouse dies and your children or grandkids inherit your IRA, they'll have to pay the taxes on it within one to five years. More importantly, they stand to lose up to 50% to 70% of the IRA due to taxes.

Instead of leaving your children and grandchildren with this burden, you could decide to create a "stretch IRA." This would allow your kids and grandkids to defer taxes on the balance of your IRA so they can create a consistent income over their lifetime.

With a stretch IRA, your beneficiaries can turn a modest account of thousands of dollars into millions of dollars by deferring taxes on it instead of paying the taxes within one to five years. And should your kids or grandkids want to accelerate the distribution or take it all out right away, they can do that as well. Or if you are worried that your 21-year-old grandson will blow it all during his first year of college, you can limit the distribution so it comes out slowly over time.

This can literally turn an IRA into millions of dollars and create a lifetime income and a family legacy while saving tens of thousands of dollars in taxes. The stretch IRA is simple to implement, but you need to put the proper paperwork in place now. So if you are interested, ask your advisor if this is appropriate for you.

By the way, 401(k)s and 403(b)s are not allowed to use this strategy. So if you have a 401(k) or 403(b), get in touch with a qualified advisor as soon as possible to explore your options.

THE ROTH IRA

A few years ago, Congress created the Roth IRA. As you probably know, the great thing about Roth IRAs is that they grow tax-free throughout your lifetime. But did you know you could extend that? If you combine a Roth IRA with a stretch IRA, it will be tax-free not only in your lifetime, but also throughout your children's and grandchildren's lives as well, if set up properly.

But there is a catch; if you convert a traditional IRA to a Roth IRA, you have to pay the conversion tax up front. When the Roth IRA first started, you were able to spread out the conversion taxes over four years — but not anymore. So if you move $100,000 from your regular IRA to your Roth IRA, you'll have to pay taxes (how much will depend on your tax bracket) and that amount will be due as soon as you move it.

But as with any problem, there is a solution. In this situation, you could utilize a little-known tax option that allows you to take a discount on the conversion of up to 59%. How? By utilizing the "Smart Asset Income Ladder" program. And while you may not have heard of this, your advisor should know how it works. Wouldn't you prefer to pay tax on only 41% of your IRA, as compared to all of it?

These kinds of tax solutions can make a big difference in your federal income tax, but you need your advisor's input and advice to determine which of these techniques will help you write a smaller check to Uncle Sam each April.

And that means your advisor should look over your tax return! If your advisor isn't aware of these techniques, you need to find one who is!

WHY ISN'T MY ACCOUNTANT TELLING ME THIS STUFF?

A lot of people ask, "Why hasn't my CPA told me about all this?" It's a fair question and one I'd ask if

I learned I could save money on taxes.

SMART ASSET INCOME LADDER

- Pulls out up to 59% of your IRA tax-free

- Reduces your taxes by more than half

- Guarantees you future income

- Works by using the tax code in your favor (IRS Sec. 1.401(a) (9) 6 and Sec. 54.4974-2)

Whenever you file your taxes, be it a 1040 or other form, there are two signature lines. One is for you, and the other is for your *tax preparer* (not tax advisor). You are paying this individual to look over last year's information, plug in the correct numbers, do all of the math, and keep you out of trouble. You aren't paying a tax preparer for advice (although many people make the mistake of believing that they are).

As you probably realize, tax preparers make most of their money during the months of February, March, and April. That's because it's "tax season," and they're preparing tons of tax returns. They know that the more people they file taxes for, the more money they make.

Now, imagine that it's March 20, and your preparer is swamped with clients and tax forms to complete. It's three in the morning, and they are burning the midnight oil. The preparer begins working on your 1040.

"You know what?" they say to themselves, "I think Mr. Smith could benefit from this tax-reduction strategy. But I'm not sure about all of the details, so I'd better grab a few books and do some research to make sure. It shouldn't take more than a couple of hours to figure out. If I'm still not sure, I can always go online and figure it out with some additional research."

DO YOU REALLY THINK THEY WOULD DO THAT?

What's the likelihood of that happening? Not much. Your preparer is paid to prepare your taxes, not save you money in the process. And when time is precious during tax season, your preparer is concerned with getting your form done and moving on to the next client, not looking out for you.

Now I have nothing against accountants. In fact, I have a very good one, and I could not live without him. But I certainly don't rely on him to reduce my tax bill. It's not his job. You are responsible for lowering your tax bill, and if you need help, you should ask your financial advisor – not your tax preparer.

WHO IS RESPONSIBLE FOR LOWERING YOUR TAXES?

If you aren't doing these things with your advisor every year, then you have to ask yourself, "why not?" Either your advisor doesn't know how to help you or he or she doesn't care. And in my book, it doesn't matter which is true. If they aren't helping me, I need to find someone who can.

Everyone is different when it comes to how much they can save in taxes. My personal record is saving a client $24,000 a year. That's $240,000 over 10 years. How great would that be?!?

That's the high end of the scale, though. Most of my clients fall in the $2,000 to $4,000 range when it comes to annual tax savings. But even so, imagine what you could do with an extra $2,000 to $4,000 per year. That's $20,000 to $40,000 in ten years. The things we are talking about are worth tens of thousands of dollars in the long run. You could buy a new car with those savings or pay for a grandchild's college education!

Of course if you are using your tax savings, who's really paying for that car or your grandchild's college? The IRS...because it's money you would have had to pay them otherwise. So be informed and take advantage of your situation.

As we discussed in this chapter, you should recognize that you need to find a problem before it becomes a problem. You've also learned:

- Municipal bonds aren't tax-free if you are in the middle-income category and are drawing Social Security.

- About the tax problems with mutual funds – things like turnover ratio and phantom income.

- How to stretch your beneficiaries and why you should consider a painless Roth IRA.

- The strength of tax-deferral.

- About insurance companies that pay taxes for you and why you should not have variable annuities inside your IRA.

But most importantly, you've learned that if your financial advisor is not telling you about these things, it's because he or she doesn't know about them or simply doesn't care. And if you are in that situation, you need to find one who does know and who does care.

So no matter what your financial situation, there is bound to be something in this chapter you can use. Next, we're going to look at long-term care planning.

CHAPTER 6

LONG-TERM CARE PLANNING

L ET'S SHIFT GEARS AND TAKE a look at the fastest growing
problem of the retired population: Healthcare, and more
specifically long-term care. Of course, every senior investor
knows about long-term care and what it entails. But if you need long-
term care, who is going to pay for it?

A year of long-term care now costs $76,680 per year[4], which isn't
small potatoes. Do you really think that your health insurance will
cover everything? Think again, and read your policy.

Do you think your HMO will cover you? It won't.

Do you think Medicare will cover you? It will for the first 20 days.
After that, you are on your own.

You may not realize it, but long-term care is the greatest unfunded liability in America. So who pays for it?

Well, if we break it down:

- 5% of the time it's paid for by LTC insurance

- 35% percent of LTC costs are paid by the individual receiving the care

- 60% of the time Medicaid picks up the tab (the first 20 days are completely paid for, but after that you have to be broke for Medicaid to step in and pay anything past the first 20 days)

The two biggest payers of long-term care, therefore, are you (the person needing LTC) and Medicaid (after you go broke). You can imagine what kind of impact this has on a couple's finances and investments.

Have you, or someone you know, ever written a monthly check for the long-term care of a loved one? It's staggering. There are individuals who regularly write out monthly checks for $6,600, $7,000, even $8,500. That's for one month of long-term care—just thirty days!

Now imagine how long your nest egg would last if you had to write checks of that size every month. You may have spent 40 years building up your savings, but you could lose it all in a few years.

Listen to what others are saying:

- According to *Business Week* magazine, nursing home care can blow apart the retirement you saved for through the years.

- The *Atlanta Journal* says that the quickest way for your family to lose your property, possessions and money is to ignore LTC and estate planning.

- AARP says that long-term care costs $50,000 a year. And with an average annual inflation rate of 5%, long-term care costs will rise to well over $100,000 per year in 10 years.

- Lastly, the American Health Care Association says that failure to prepare for the cost of long-term care is the primary cause of poverty among the elderly.

WHO NEEDS IT?

Your spouse does! Because if they get ill, you are going to be the one holding the bag! The majority of seniors in this country are not only gambling with their investments, but with their health as well. And if you don't have long-term care insurance, you are also gambling with your future. Are you willing to risk everything you've worked and saved for in hopes that you won't ever need long-term care?

About 60% of those reading this book will spend less than $100,000 in long-term care. They are the lucky ones.

About 30% of readers will spend between $100,000 and $500,000 on long-term care[5]. That may seem like a lot...

But 10% of those reading this book will spend more than $500,000 on long-term care! And if you don't have the money for long-term care, the government will cover the cost for you, but only after you or your spouse reaches the poverty level by spending all of your life savings. Of course, there is no way of knowing which of these categories you will fall in. And since none of us know how much we'll spend in long-term care, we can do one of two things – either cross our fingers or get long-term care insurance.

Obviously, you don't want to be one of those people who spend a half-a-million dollars on long-term care or go broke trying. No one does. But statistics show that 10% of seniors will spend that much. So it's better to plan for long-term care and purchase LTC insurance than to hope for the best and cross your fingers. If you don't plan, you will be relying on the government for care...and we've already seen how poorly they look out for us when it comes to taxes.

WHO SELLS LTC INSURANCE AND WHY?

About a million people in the US have bought long-term care insurance[6]. Of course, more people are buying long-term care insurance each day, but the number of people who own it remains relatively constant because as more people age and buy LTC others who already own LTC are dying.

The rest of the population has long-term care insurance through the government...and if you think that's enough take a look at how it works.

The government will pay for your long-term care only if you meet certain criteria, which means you must have exhausted every financial asset you own before they chip in a cent -- and that literally means everything.

For example, in Minnesota if you have a spouse, the government will allow you to keep your house until you die. If you are single, you are allowed to keep your house for six months before you must sell it to cover your care. The government also allows you to keep your car and $1,500 in burial funds. If you have a burial trust, you are allowed to put as much as you want in it, but that money must be used for your burial. If you are single, you can keep $3,000 in cash and investments, and married couples can keep $6,000[7]. Lastly, you are allowed to keep a family bible.

That's it. But some of you might be thinking that your life insurance will solve your problem. It might, but there's a problem with that solution.

Some people say, "I've got $250,000 in life insurance. So if I go into a long-term care facility, spend a lot of money and die, my wife and children will get the $250,000."

That's not how the system works. If you need long-term care, the government will require you to spend the cash value of your life insurance before they'll take care of you. So what happens in those situations? You spend all of the cash value of your life insurance on long-term care, and your spouse and children end up with nothing when you are gone.

The government doesn't make exceptions or have loopholes when it comes to long-term care. A prenuptial agreement won't protect your assets. Your 401(k) and other retirement accounts have to be used, as well as things like revocable living trusts. So don't fall for any claims that certain investments or shelters will be left alone.

Let's say Jim and Mary live in Minnesota and have $300,000 in investments, as well as their house and car. Jim needs long-term care, and Mary is forced to spend $294,000 of their investments before they qualify for any government assistance (remember, a married couple can only keep $6,000).

Mary still has $6,000 in her investments, but how much peace of mind would she have once her nest egg went from $300,000 to $6,000? Not much, because a few problems or repairs can wipe that out. If Mary needs a new car, or she needs a new furnace for the house, or a storm causes some damage to her home, or the roof needs some repairs... anything like that could wipe Mary out!

LTC insurance was designed to make sure something like that couldn't happen to you. But there are a couple of problems with LTC insurance.

LTC insurance is not only expensive, but your premiums will almost certainly increase. And if you can't afford your premiums 10 years down the road, you'll have to cancel your coverage.

What happens then? You don't get your money back. And if you die without needing LTC your beneficiaries certainly don't get your money. When it comes to long-term care insurance, you either use it or lose it.

10 SECRETS YOUR LONG-TERM CARE SALESPERSON DOESN'T WANT YOU TO KNOW

Everyone should consider long-term care insurance, but it is expensive and not everyone qualifies because of their health. So if you are thinking about LTC insurance, make sure you protect yourself. The following list will not only make you an informed consumer, but also help you separate the handful of long-term care advisors out there from all the long-term care salespeople you are likely to meet.

_____

1. "Don't ask me this question!"

There is one question every long-term care salesperson doesn't want you to ask:

"What are the last three books you read about long-term care issues?"

You can imagine what you might hear: "Well, I went through the book the company I'm selling for gave me when I spent a day in their training class."

But that's not good enough. Would you really give your money to someone who hasn't read at least three books on the very topic of the product they are selling? Anyone who isn't knowledgeable about long-term care, but tries to tell you that their LTC insurance is best is nothing more than a salesperson.

2. "The more you buy, the more I make."

People with different financial situations are buying the same amount of LTC insurance all the time, and it doesn't make sense. Talk to someone with $500,000 in assets and $70,000 of income, then to someone with $100,000 of assets and $20,000 of income, and both were probably sold the exact same amount of long-term care insurance.

Yet someone with $500,000 in assets and $70,000 of income shouldn't need the same amount of coverage as someone with $100,000 and $20,000 of income. That's because the person with more assets and income should be able to pay a little bit of their own long-term care cost without making much of a financial sacrifice. And if they can do that, shouldn't they be paying less because they don't need as much LTC insurance? Of course!

You probably don't have a zero deductible on your car insurance, right? And why? Because you can afford to pay a few hundred dollars out of pocket for an accident or repair, and it's worth it to save the money on your auto insurance. Well, your LTC insurance should be the same way.

But long-term care salespeople don't tell you this because they'd lose commissions if you bought a lesser policy. If a long-term care salesperson admitted that you only needed $50 of coverage a day versus $100 of coverage, they'd only make half the commission. So if someone tries to sell you a policy without even looking at your assets, expenses, and tax return, you can bet they're a salesperson.

3. "I only recommend one company."

Imagine that you're a farmer and you need to buy a new automobile. You are looking for a truck to haul feed and tools that has four-wheel drive to get through the snow and mud of country roads.

But what if you walked into a car dealer that only sold one kind of European sports car? What if the car dealer showed you the car and said, "Well, it's got four wheels, a trunk, and steering wheel. It's what you need." You'd probably turn around and walk out as soon as you realized that there were no trucks in the showroom.

So then why is it okay when advisors only sell one particular product from a certain company? If someone tells you they only offer one type of long-term care policy from one company, would you buy it without shopping around? Hopefully not.

4. "Your premium will go up."

No one is going to mention that your long-term care premiums can go up unless you ask. And even then, they may suggest that it's possible, but wave off your concerns.

Remember that companies can and will increase your premiums in the future, and if you can't afford your premiums, you'll lose your coverage...and you won't get your money back.

5. "The company is new at this."

Just like you wouldn't get in a taxi driven by a 16 year-old, you should avoid companies that are new to LTC insurance. Odds are that companies that have never offered long-term care policies before now have no idea how to set rates and manage them in the future. This means that new companies will have to change their rates and benefits as they learn from their mistakes, which translates into increased premiums for you down the road as well as other headaches.

6. "What you don't know won't hurt you."

How many times have we all heard that? If someone is trying to sell you LTC insurance, but avoids explaining things by telling you, "It's a complicated issue," you should beware. When this happens, either the salesperson doesn't understand it themselves or the policy will obviously be a bad choice. Either way, it's not a good sign. If they can't explain everything about the LTC insurance they are offering, go to someone who can. Make sure you understand a policy before you buy it.

7. "I can save you 15% to 30% on your premiums."

This is something you aren't likely to hear. Even if you bought your LTC insurance years ago, you could still save 15% to 30% of your premiums. But few people will tell you this or even know how to do it.

8. "Your premiums are deductible."

It's true, but only if you become so sick that you are spending 7.5% of your income on medical expenses. Of course, once that happens, you wouldn't be eligible for long-term care from any company. Besides, even if you were, you wouldn't have money to buy LTC insurance because every last cent would be spent on the care itself.

9. "You can compare long-term care companies yourself."

This is something else you aren't likely to hear. There is actually software available that allows you to compare LTC policies side-by-side, and you should do just that before you buy long-term care insurance.

10. "There are other ways to protect your assets without buying long-term care insurance."

This is also something you'll never hear from someone trying to sell you LTC insurance. Not everyone qualifies for long-term care insurance. But if you need coverage, there is a way to protect your assets without buying LTC insurance.

You should be shown how to do this, as well as alternatives to buying LTC insurance. But if the person selling you a policy doesn't mention these options, they are a salesperson and not an advisor.

Another option we've already mentioned is the government plan for coverage: Medicaid.

Medicaid is an entitlement program covered by Social Security. If you've paid into Social Security you may qualify for Medicaid. But as with everything involving the government, you have to understand the rules in order to receive your benefits.

Medicaid is the "Cadillac" of all policies and pays 100% of all nursing home costs including medications. But the only way you get to ride this Cadillac is if you are flat broke like we talked about earlier. You must meet the eligibility requirements. As with the example of Jim and Mary, you must already have spent all of your savings and investments (even your IRA's and retirement plans) for long-term care in order to qualify.

So what can you do? Well, don't give up. If you can't afford long-term care insurance or your loved one is already in a long-term care facility, you aren't completely out of luck. There are things you can do such as "half-a-loaf planning" or "name-on-the check" strategies. But you need professional help.

WHAT DO YOU CALL A GOOD LAWYER?

You shouldn't seek just any old attorney to help you with this. They must be elder law specialists, because very few attorneys understand the issues and complex rules that pertain to long-term care.

ARE THERE MEDICAID FRIENDLY INVESTMENTS?

There is an investment that in some instances will protect you from Medicaid "spend-down". It's called a Medicaid-friendly annuity, and these are extremely specialized annuities. There are hundreds of annuities out there, but almost none of them have the specific language required to ensure that a long-term care stay will not require it to be spent. The rules and regulations for these annuities vary from state to state, and you shouldn't just assume any annuities you own will protect you.

Your advisor or financial consultant may tell you that you have a Medicaid-friendly annuity. But if they do, ask them to prove it by showing it to you in writing. If they can't prove it in writing, then that annuity isn't protected – no matter what they tell you.

It's better to find out that your annuity isn't protected before there is a problem. Remember, there are very few Medicaid-friendly annuities in existence, so make sure you sit down with a competent professional to discuss this option.

Let's take a moment and look at how these annuities work.

Remember Mary and Jim? They had $300,000 in investments, but when Jim needed long-term care, Mary was forced to spend $294,000. She only ended up keeping $6,000 – just enough for a few home repairs.

Well, let's say that Jim and Mary had their $300,000 in a Medicaid-friendly annuity. If that were the case, Mary would be in control of her finances. She could choose to spend as much of the $300,000 as she wanted on Jim's long-term care, or she could elect to keep as much of the $300,000 as she wanted. Mary would have peace of mind.

But proceed with caution! This type of planning is very compli-cated, and you do not want to make a mistake. It is absolutely crucial you work with a professional who knows what they are doing and is familiar with Medicaid-friendly annuities.

WHAT IF I CAN'T GET LTC INSURANCE?

Unfortunately, Jim and Mary's dilemma is typical of a lot of people. Most seniors don't have enough assets to self-insure, and they have too many assets to qualify for Medicaid. Yet they can't afford LTC insurance or don't qualify for it because of their health. So what if you can't get LTC insurance and don't qualify for Medicaid?

One thing you can do is make yourself eligible for Medicaid with-out going broke paying for long-term care. It is possible to qualify for Medicaid in many states without becoming impoverished by imple-menting an asset protection plan. An asset protection plan protects your financial assets from Medicaid-required spending, catastrophic illness, creditors, and qualifies an institutionalized individual for Medicaid immediately. In other words, if you are already in a nursing home and paying out of pocket for your care, you can still qualify for Medicaid immediately and protect your remaining assets.

But the government is currently trying to change this type of plan to keep people from taking advantage of it. So regardless of whether you currently need long-term care or not, get and remain informed. Remember the Navy and the stress test of the ship's chains? It's always better to plan before problems arise.

Best of all, this kind of planning is completely legal. This is not a loophole, but your right under state and federal laws as they are written right now. It's part of the rule book; you just have to know about it.

Now that you better understand why long-term care is so important, let's look at legal planning.

CHAPTER 7

LEGAL PLANNING

ANOTHER WAY TO PROTECT YOUR hard-earned money is through legal planning. And as with everything else we've discussed, there are areas of legal planning that you've probably already put some thought into, like inheritances and estates. But there still may be things your advisor hasn't told you...things like:

- How a medical directive is different than a living will or medical power of attorney...or...

- How to avoid probate without a trust.

As you'll soon realize, no one's told you the whole truth about legal planning...no matter how much you think you know.

THE INDUSTRY DOESN'T GIVE YOU THE WHOLE TRUTH

You may realize that probate isn't the best way to pass along your money after you are gone. And you may realize that there are two types of probate: the kind that you go through while you're alive and that which occurs when you die. But no matter which kind of probate you are familiar with, you'll be happy to know that no investment ever has to go through any kind of probate. Better yet, you don't need to set up an expensive trust to avoid probate. In fact, avoiding probate is as easy as correctly titling your stocks, bonds, mutual funds, CD's, and bank accounts. By making sure everything is correctly titled, nothing you own will go into any kind of probate. And it costs you nothing to make this happen.

Obviously, no one wants their assets to go through probate – not you, not me, not your friends...no one. It's no secret that probate is a four-letter word that should be avoided at all costs. But if that's true, shouldn't your advisor already know that you don't want your assets to go through probate? And if he or she knows it, why hasn't he or she addressed this issue with you?

Remember, avoiding probate is both free and easy! If you go to your advisor and say, "I don't want my assets to go through probate," he or she is going to pull out a special form and have you fill it out. On the form, you'll have to indicate who you want your assets to go to, but once you fill it out and sign it, that's it. No legal headaches, no waiting, no setting up estates. It's done.

By the way, you can do the same thing at your bank. If you go to your banker and tell them you don't want your assets and accounts going through probate, they are going to have you fill out the exact same form.

WHY DON'T YOUR BANKERS AND ADVISORS WANT YOU TO KNOW THIS?

Since your banker and broker know that no one wants their assets to go through probate, why hasn't something already been done? If these forms are so easy to fill out and don't cost anything, why hasn't your broker already told you about them?

It's a simple answer: They want to keep your money at their firm as long as possible. The average probate lasts two or three years (and many last longer than that). And while your money is in probate, it stays right in your bank and brokerage accounts. Therefore, even when you're gone, your advisor and bank continue to make money off your assets.

If you haven't already done so, tell your advisor that you don't want your assets to go through probate. Better yet, take your assets to an advisor who knows and cares about your best interests.

After all, there are really only three reasons an advisor wouldn't already have done this for all of his or her clients:

- They didn't know about the form
- They didn't care that their clients might have to spend years in probate
- They intentionally withheld the information to have a chance at keeping the accounts longer

And none of those are good reasons!

INHERITANCE...A GOOD OR BAD THING?

Like a lot of investors, many seniors lost their bearings during the Internet boom of the 1990's. But thanks to the recent downturns of the past few years, we've all been brought back to our senses. The "get everything you can" attitude of the 1990's has given way to a realization that not all of us are in the accumulation period of our lives. Depending on your age and situation, you are either:

- Preserving your assets...or...

- Spending them to enjoy yourself

The truth is that your generation is a generation of savers, and you should feel proud of yourself for all of your hard work. But you also have one big problem: You have raised a generation of spenders. We've all heard how younger generations spend, spend, spend, and have saved next- to-nothing for retirement. If you ask me, this sounds like a problem waiting to happen. And that means that it's time for a stress test!

Have you ever noticed how some people suddenly treat their parents differently once they turn 65? Maybe it hasn't happened to you personally, but a lot of seniors have had to deal with adult children who think that turning 65 means you suddenly take a "stupid pill" when it comes to money and that you can't think for yourself.

It's pretty ridiculous, especially once you put things into perspective. For example, here's Debbie, a retired widow with her house paid in full, no debt, $300,000 in investments, and a nice $20,000 nest egg in her checking account (just in case). Debbie loves her son, Steve, so she loans him a few thousand dollars every year. Yet Steve has started asking her about her financial matters, bullying her with his opinion, even when she doesn't ask for it. Steve, of course, is sitting with a $300,000 mortgage, $40,000 of car debt, $40,000 in his 401(k), $10,000 in credit card debt, and absolutely no savings. And he just borrowed $5,000 from his mother last week...but now he insists he knows what's best for her money.

If you know anyone whose children treat them like this, be sure to give them some moral support, because they need it. Remind them which generation built this country and which is spending it away.

IT'S NO JOKE

By the way, what is a seven-letter word your children use for financial planning? Inherit.

It sounds like a great joke, but it's not. Ask your children what you should do with your money, and they'll tell you to spend it. And you'd better believe them...because if you don't spend your money – they will!

You may have driven the same car for 15 years because it was still in good shape. But what will happen once your children inherit your money? They'll head down to the Lexus dealer and buy a brand new luxury car with a leather interior. And you know that cruise around the world you and your spouse never took because it was just too expensive? Well, once you leave your children their inheritance, it's "Hello, Disney World!"

So, if there is something you really want to do, but haven't done because it's too expensive, do it anyway. Treat yourself. It's your money. You've worked hard to save it, so aren't you entitled to enjoy it?

We all know that you can't take it with you. And unless you use some of your savings to enjoy yourself, it's going to end up in one of three places: your children's bank account, the nursing home, or the IRS. And since you're responsible for the risks you take with your money, shouldn't you also be responsible for the rewards?

A client once told me that he wants the last check he writes to be to the undertaker. And he wants it to bounce! That's a great mentality to have!

YOUR FINANCES CONSIST OF MORE THAN YOUR MONEY

If you ask a bunch of people how they are doing financially, you'll get a wide range of answers. Some will tell you they are doing great...that they *made* a 15% return last year. Others will tell you they are doing lousy...that they *lost* 15% last year.

But do returns have anything to do with how you're doing financially?

Returns are certainly important, but great returns alone don't mean that you are doing fine financially. That 15% return you made last year doesn't matter much if you gave a big chunk of it to Uncle Sam, spent all of it on long-term care costs, or if your return was eaten up by probate and estate costs. So while your returns are important, they amount to nothing if you don't take care of your affairs. If you

> The old adage is true: the one who takes care of the money dies first! So begin your legal planning immediately, and explain everything to your spouse.

leave everything in chaos when you die, your surviving spouse will not only spend all those returns you've bragged about, but more. And with all the stress involved in cleaning up investments and accounts, not to mention taxes and other problems, he or she will probably be on the verge of a breakdown.

GIVE YOUR SPOUSE YOUR JOHN HANCOCK

Conservatorship probate (the probate that occurs while the person is still living) is more frustrating and difficult than going through probate at death.

Let's say that John's finances end up in conservatorship probate. John, who is married to Elaine, has come down with Alzheimer's, is no longer mentally capable of taking care of himself, and is unable to function. Since John has lost his legal capacity to think and act for himself, he needs more care than Elaine can provide. With John in a nursing home, Elaine wants to sell their house and move into a condominium which requires no maintenance.

But without John's signature, she's unable to sell the house. And because of his condition, John can't sign the necessary papers to sell the house. That means Elaine is stuck in a difficult situation.

This scenario can apply to anything...homes, IRAs, stock accounts—anything with John's name on it would essentially be frozen.

What Elaine needs is a durable power of attorney... a legal document that allows someone else to act on your behalf should you become incapacitated or unable to function. If John had named Elaine as his power of attorney, she'd be able to take care of everything.

If you and your spouse don't have a power of attorney, getting one should be the first thing on your to-do list tomorrow. Because if you find yourself in a situation similar to Elaine and John, you'll have to jump through a lot of hoops to get things straightened out. You'd have to be appointed conservator of your own spouse. That would mean hiring an attorney, paying several thousands of dollars in legal fees, and going before the court to be appointed as your spouse's conservator. Once that's done, the court will be looking over your shoulder every time you make a decision to ensure that you are spending your money appropriately.

Yet you can avoid all of this just by paying an attorney $50 to $100 to get a power of attorney done. But you can't get a power of attorney after you are incapacitated, so do it now. Remember the Navy stress test: fix things before they become problems.

WHOSE JOB IS IT TO MAKE SURE YOUR POWER OF ATTORNEY IS UP TO DATE?

Powers of Attorney deal mostly with your money. And who handles your money and your investments? Your financial advisor. While an attorney needs to draft the initial document, your financial advisor should make sure that it is up-to-date and reflects any changes in your financial situation.

MEDICAL POWERS OF ATTORNEY

But even if you have a financial power of attorney, that's not enough. You need to make sure you have a power of attorney for medical purposes... and more importantly a Quality of Life Directive. Unlike a living will, a Quality of Life Directive is a lot more comprehensive and in-depth.

Quality of Life Directives actually tell your loved ones how you want to be taken care of medically when you can't tell them yourself. How much pain control would you want? Would you want to be taken off life support? What if you were in a coma?

These are all very difficult questions, but you need to take the time to answer them. Otherwise the decisions will be taken out of your hands.

Fortunately, Quality of Life Directives cover just about every possible scenario you'd need to consider. Best of all, you can get them free from a number of places: your doctor, your hospital, online...you can even get them from a qualified senior advisor.

But it's not enough just to have a Quality of Life Directive. You need to have it with you in the event of an emergency. In fact, five out of ten people who have a medical power of attorney don't have it with them when they show up at the hospital for care. That's because no one carries it around with them. Most of us understand just how important a Quality of Life Directive is, so we put it in a safety deposit box or somewhere secure for safekeeping.

After all, do you stick your Quality of Life Directive in your pocket when you drive to the store for a few things? Probably not.

But let's say you go outside one Sunday afternoon to play with your grandkids, and you begin to have chest pains. You are having a heart attack, so your son or daughter rushes you to the hospital.

When you arrive at the hospital, the first thing the staff will do is shove a clipboard in your face to sign. And what's on that clipboard? A piece of paper that makes the hospital your power of attorney. And by signing it, all the good work you've done has been eliminated. It's done to protect the hospital, not you, so you need to have your Quality of Life directive with you.

And since it's not convenient to carry it around at all times, there's an alternative. You can get a laminated card for your wallet that gives the hospital a number to call to obtain your medical power of attorney electronically. EMTs and hospital staff are sure to find it, since they check the patient's wallet or purse for a driver's license, identification, and insurance cards. If you have this card with those things, they'll see it and be able to obtain your Quality of Life Directive on demand.

In order to get one of these cards, your Quality of Life Directive must be electronically filed. If you don't have one, ask your financial advisor to help you get one. If they say they can't get one, you'd better find someone who can. One day your life may depend on it!

A Quality of Life Directive is the best gift you can give your loved ones. It's hard to know what we want to do with our own bodies, but it's even harder to decide what to do with someone else's body. So get this done if you love your family!

BENEFICIARY PLANNING

Another thing that's extremely important is the correct designation of your beneficiaries. Throughout my years in the financial services business, **I've found that almost 99% of all people have their beneficiaries incorrectly designated.** When this happens, not only are grandchildren and family members accidentally disinherited, but families lose the hard-earned money you left them.

Look at Frank and his wife, Sarah. Frank and Sarah have three sons, and each son has a son of his own. In other words, Frank and Sarah have three sons and three grandsons.

If Frank dies, Sarah gets the couple's money. Easy enough, right? Then once Sarah dies, it goes to the sons and grandsons according to her wishes.

But what if one of their sons dies before either Frank or Sarah? Who are the beneficiaries in that situation?

At first, it doesn't seem like much of a problem. Most people indicate that their inheritance should be split evenly between all their children. That makes sense, as long as all of your children outlive you. But if one of Frank and Sarah's sons die before they do, a grandson gets left out. By indicating that their money should be split evenly among their sons, half of Frank and Sarah's money would go to each of their two living sons. And in the process, they'd leave out the grandson who needed the money most – the one who lost his father.

And that's not the only scenario. Even if Frank and Sarah prepared for the death of one of their sons, other things could happen. For example, let's say that one of Frank and Sarah's sons died, but they set up their wills so that each surviving son gets one third of their money, and the grandson who lost his father gets a third.

Sounds grea... unless family quarrels and divorce enter the picture. Suppose that one of Frank and Sarah's surviving sons divorces his wife after they've inherited Frank and Sarah's money. What happens if their daughter-in-law is given the money in the divorce, then runs off and marries a lazy jerk who gambles it all away? Now Frank and Sarah have not only disinherited their divorced son, but a third of their money as well.

You may think you are fine because you've thought all this out in your will. If so, good for you...but you are still at risk for these kinds of problems.

Why? Because not everything is covered by your will. In fact, the vast majority of most people's assets don't go through their wills. Things such as life insurance, IRAs, 401(k)s, and annuities do not go through wills. And if you are like most retired investors, where is the bulk of your money? In your life insurance, your IRA, your 401(k), and your annuities. So even if your will states that your grandchildren will get their college tuition paid thanks to you, it won't happen if the money is in your IRA.

Many seniors designate their kids as joint owners of their investments and accounts. This is a dangerous situation to be in, because their actions put your money at risk. Let's say that you and your daughter have joint ownership of all the stocks in your portfolio, and that she was just involved in a car accident. Your daughter is okay, but is sued by one of the other drivers involved. As part of the lawsuit, that individual could go after your portfolio simply because your daughter's name is listed as a co-owner.

AND IT'S NOT ALWAYS ACCIDENTS AND GREED THAT CAUSE THESE KINDS OF PROBLEMS

I once knew a brother and sister who didn't have any other living relatives. The brother had $300,000 in investments, while the sister had

$100,000. They intended to look out for each other, so they pooled their money into one joint account.

Sadly, the sister became ill and needed long-term care. And as we discussed earlier, Medicaid doesn't cover long-term care until you are broke. So not only did the sister have to spend her $100,000 on her long-term care, but her brother's money was used as well. By setting up a joint account with his sister, the brother's assets dwindled from $300,000 to just $3,000 – the amount Medicare allowed him to keep.

As you can see, in an effort to solve one problem many people find they've created another. So you need to know the whole picture before you make any changes.

No one willingly disinherits family members they love, but it is possible for accidents like these to take your money away from the people you want to have it. So now is the time to stress test your beneficiary designations, because once you're gone, there isn't anything you can do.

CHAPTER 8

WHAT THE FINANCIAL INDUSTRY DOESN'T WANT YOU TO KNOW

WILL ROGERS' FAMOUS QUIP IS as true today as the day he first said it. As a retired investor, this is the attitude you need to have when it comes to your finances. Unlike pre-retirement investors, you don't have 20 or 30 years to get back any money you lose.

> "I am more concerned with the return of my principal, rather than the return on my principal."
>
> — *WILL ROGERS ACTOR / AUTHOR / PHILANTHROPIST*

We've already mentioned that you should be out of the accumulation period and into the preservation period (or better yet, the spending period) of your life. But as you'll soon learn, the financial services industry doesn't look out for people who want to preserve their wealth. They're too busy trying to force people to accumulate more money.

A BRIEF HISTORY OF SAVING

It used to be that when people needed to invest their money, they went to their bank. Some of us used savings accounts. We could buy bonds and other types of low-risk investments from our banker. Of course, we can still do that, but things have certainly changed.

As you probably remember, there was a time in this country when you could walk into your local bank, say hello to the manager, and he'd offer you a cup of coffee and chat with you awhile. Not anymore. Today, banks are like musical chairs. The teller who was there last week is gone. The manager sits in an office with his or her door closed. Even the names of banks change on a regular basis as mergers and buyouts have caused local and regional banks to all but disappear.

And it's not just the banks themselves that have changed. Our whole notion of banks has changed. No longer do rates subtly change over a period of time; look at Certificates of Deposit. The rates on CDs have gone down in recent years...and at an alarming rate. It doesn't surprise us that the rates were quick to go down, but they've been slow to go back up.

And what about the Federal Deposit Insurance Corporation (FDIC)? Remember when they ran out of money in 1991 and almost ran out again in 2008? Unless you read Banking Industry trade journals you may not have even been aware of this. If this comes as a surprise to you, don't be too hard on yourself. After all, how could you have known that it happened when lobbyists work to keep it out of the news?

In 1991, the media was too busy covering the Savings and Loan bankruptcy to pay any attention to the FDIC. So while newspapers and television focused on thousands of Savings and Loans across the country running out of money, the FDIC itself was almost belly-up. In hindsight, it's probably a good thing the media never covered this story. If they had, it could have sparked a panic that would have turned the 1990's from a boom to a bust.

Think about it: if the FDIC had become news in 1991, you would have headed down to your bank and taken every last dollar out of your accounts. A lot of people would have done that. But can you imagine the impact that kind of panic would have had on our country? There would have been lines of people waiting to take everything out of their bank accounts all across the country! If that had happened, we would have had more than Savings and Loan problems; regular banks would have gone bankrupt as well.

And most people would not have gotten their money back. That's because banks don't keep 100% of their funds on hand. Banks keep only $10.00 in their safes for every $100 they have on deposit[8]. And FDIC insurance only adds $1.35 to that total[9]. That's a whopping $11.35 backing up your $100.

It's certainly not much, but we don't worry about it because our money is safe in the bank, right?

It is as long as we continue to believe in them. Then again, 322 banks went under from 2008-2010.[10]

This is not to suggest that you should stop believing in the security and safety of banks. Banks are great places to hold your money, but you need to be aware of how they work and what kind of protection you actually have.

As you already know, the stock market has become an attractive alternative to banks when it comes to saving and investing for the future, especially now that technology like the Internet has made it easier for everyday people to buy and sell stocks easily and cheaply. In the past 10 years, the stock market has become a national pastime of sorts. No longer is it just for the wealthy and money-conscious investors. Many of us have moved away from banks and toward stocks as a way of preparing for the future; we are trading some of the safety we had at the bank for the possibility of a higher return on our investment.

Because of this, many investors want to know the average rate of return for the stock market. After all, we're told that the average return should justify our confidence in Wall Street and remind us that our money is safe, right?

But just what is the average rate of return for the stock market? Is it 10%? 5%? 20%?

Well, the truth is that all of those numbers are correct...depending on the time period you are talking about. From 1976 to 1986 the average rate of return was 21%. From 1961 to 1971 it was 11%, and from 1964 to 1974 it was 4%. And over a 65-year period, the average rate of return is about 8%.

Is that 8% average less than you expected? Does it make you nervous or less confident in the stock market?

In fact, it shouldn't make a difference to you because a 65 year average wouldn't pertain to you.   After all, who retires for 65 years? No one! So how does that average rate of return impact you? Not in the least.

THE BIG LIE (AVERAGE RATE OF RETURN)

The bottom line is that the average rate of return is the biggest lie you'll ever hear from the financial services industry. Every type of investment forces its average annual return on you, telling you it's a benchmark for comparison and the most important number you should be concerned with. That is simply not true.

Everyone in the financial services industry talks about how important the average rate of return is. Mutual funds use their average rate of return to convince you to buy their fund, brokers talk about the average rates of return for their firm's products, and even money magazines talk about average rates of return when comparing investments. But relying on this is misleading, and here's why:

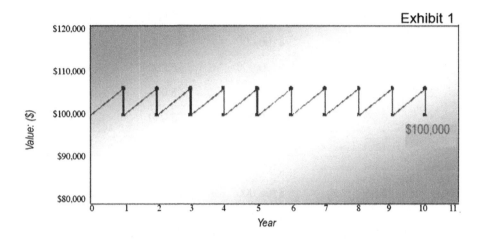

Let's say you own an investment that earns 6%. If you take 6% out of that investment, your balance in the account should remain constant. In other words, if you have $100,000 in a CD earning 6%, it goes up to $106,000. If you take out 6%, you're back to $100,000. This continues year after year, and you make a constant $6,000 without losing any money. (Exhibits 1 and 2)

Retirement Withdrawal (Assumptions) Deposit: $100,000				Exhibit 2
10 yr average return 6.0%			Withdrawal rate per year 6.0%	
Year	Rate of Return	Beginning Value ($100,000)	Withdrawal	Ending Value
1	6.0%	$100,000	$6,000	$100,000
2	6.0%	$106,000	$6,000	$100,000
3	6.0%	$106,000	$6,000	$100,000
4	6.0%	$106,000	$6,000	$100,000
5	6.0%	$106,000	$6,000	$100,000
6	6.0%	$106,000	$6,000	$100,000
7	6.0%	$106,000	$6,000	$100,000
8	6.0%	$106,000	$6,000	$100,000
9	6.0%	$106,000	$6,000	$100,000
10	6.0%	$106,000	$6,000	$100,000

Now let's compare that to another investment that also has a 6% average rate of return.   Let's say you own $100,000 of a mutual fund, and it does the following: it loses 30% of its value, then loses 20%, then makes 10%, makes another 10%, makes 10% again, makes another 10%, makes yet another 10%, makes 10% again, then makes 20%, and finally makes 30%. This would give you an average rate of return of 6% over those 10 years. (Exhibits 3 and 4)

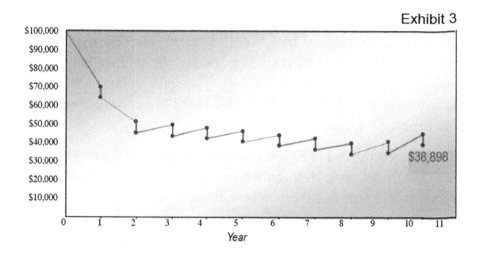

Exhibit 3

Monte Carlo — Assumptions				Exhibit 4
Deposit: $100,000				
10 yr average return 6.0%		**WIthdrawal rate per year 6.0%**		
Example A				
Year	Rate of Return	Beginning Value ($100,000)	Withdrawal	Ending Value
1	-30.0%	$70,000	$6,000	$64,000
2	-20.0%	$51,200	$6,000	$45,200
3	10.0%	$49,720	$6,000	$43,720
4	10.0%	$48,092	$6,000	$42,092
5	10.0%	$46,301	$6,000	$40,301
6	10.0%	$44,331	$6,000	$38,331
7	10.0%	$42,164	$6,000	$36,164
8	10.0%	$39,781	$6,000	$33,781
9	20.0%	$40,537	$6,000	$34,537
10	30.0%	$44,898	$6,000	$38,898

With the mutual fund, your $100,000 fell to $70,000. Of course, if you took out $6,000, you are left with $64,000. The next month, that amount would fall to $51,000, and by taking out another $6,000, you are left with $45,000. Of course, now you start making 10%, but it doesn't cover your recent withdrawals. That 10% return doesn't cover your losses and withdrawals.

In fact, by the end of 10 years, you are left with less than $39,000 – even though you made 20% and 30% in the last two years. Despite that average rate of return of 6%, you've still lost money.

But what if it goes the opposite way? Let's say the fund makes 30%, then makes 20%, before making 10% the next six years before losing 20%, then losing 30%.

In that scenario you would have $105,000 at the end of 10 years (assuming you were withdrawing $6,000 each year).

The sequence of returns makes a big difference. A bad sequence of returns hurts you a lot more on the downside than a good sequence of returns can help you on the good side.

If you start with losses you could lose more than 60% of your money. But even if you start with gains you only end up growing your account by 5% ($5,000 on your initial $100,000 investment) after 10 years. The absolute best case scenario is not much different than earning 6% in a CD. But a mildly bad scenario could be devastating to your portfolio and your lifestyle! (Exhibit 5)

Monte Carlo — Assumptions Deposit: $100,000 10 yr average return 6.0% Withdrawal rate per year 6.0%				Exhibit 5
Example B				
Year	Rate of Return	Beginning Value ($100,000)	Withdrawal	Ending Value
1	30.0%	$130,000	$6,000	$124,000
2	20.0%	$148,800	$6,000	$142,800
3	10.0%	$157,080	$6,000	$151,080
4	10.0%	$166,188	$6,000	$160,188
5	10.0%	$176,207	$6,000	$170,207
6	10.0%	$187,227	$6,000	$181,227
7	10.0%	$199,350	$6,000	$193,350
8	10.0%	$212,685	$6,000	$206,685
9	-20.0%	$165,348	$6,000	$159,348
10	-30.0%	$111,544	$6,000	$105,544

In comparison, both the CD and mutual fund had an annual rate of return of 6%, but there is a real possibility you could lose money with a fund or stocks. This is why the average rate of return is a big lie.

IS MY RETIREMENT CONTROLLING MY INVESTMENTS, OR ARE MY INVESTMENTS CONTROLLING MY RETIREMENT?

Let me explain: If the stock market goes down 30% in one year, what would you do? Would you cut back and not spend any money? If you have a nice cruise planned to Alaska, but your nest egg is suddenly cut back by 30%, would you postpone your trip?

And what happens if someone gets sick the next year? Or something happens to a family member? As we all know, any number of things can happen. Roofs start leaking, someone runs into your car, a flood ruins your basement. The next thing you know, you've delayed your trip for years.

At this point in your life, should you really be delaying your trip? Of course not! If you want to go to Alaska, you should go and not let your investments control your retirement. This really hit home for me when I was recently watching a video shot two years ago. It was a class I conducted for 26 of my clients. Since then, four of them have passed away, and their average age was only 67.

So what's more important than the average rate of return? How you get it. You have to plan for the bear as well as the bull. So, stress test your investments. If you can afford to make a withdrawal from your investments only when the market is doing well, you've got a problem. There will inevitably be times when your investments are not going to be doing well, and you need to be able to take money from your accounts then, too. And isn't it better to deal with this now than to find out you have a problem after something happens? Absolutely!

REARVIEW INVESTING

Another mistake a lot of investors make today is what's called "rearview investing". We've all heard the saying that hindsight is 20/20, but some of us take it a little too literally when it comes to the stock market.

Rearview investing is when someone chases after mutual funds or other investments because they've done well over the last year or so. If someone says, "This fund made a 285% return last year so I'm going to get into it and double my money," they are chasing yesterday's news. And as you can imagine, it's not a good idea.

The recent bull/bear market cycle provides a clear example of how harmful an undisciplined, emotional approach to investing can be. Investors poured a record $309 billion into equity mutual funds at the top of the market in 2000, purchasing shares at the highest possible price, while also pulling a record $50 billion from bond funds right before they made their meteoric rise.

A few years later, the opposite happened. Investors put a record $140 billion into bond funds in 2002, buying these bonds when interest rates brought their prices to a 45-year high. And where did they get the money to do this? By pulling a record $27 billion out of equity funds at the bottom of the market, selling at the lowest possible price. In both situations, irrational behavior led investors to do the exact opposite of what they should have done in both instances.

The Effects of Irrational Investing

Year	Stock Funds	Bond Funds	S&P 500
2000	$309 billion	(-$50 billion)	1,509 – Market High
2002	(-$27 billion)	$140 billion	776 – Market

Source: Barra.com "Mutual Fund Facts and Figures," Investment Company Institute, 2003

The exact same phenomenon happened from 2008-2011. Never use an investment's past performance as justification to get in and make money. And whatever you do, don't chase the market because you think you can land big returns in the process. A lot of investors have learned that doing so means you'll always be a day late and a dollar short – literally!

DO THEY REALLY HAVE YOUR BEST INTEREST AT HEART?

It's no surprise that a lot of investors work with financial advisors. While most of these consultants call themselves advisors, the title seldom fits.

Unfortunately the vast majority of "advisors" have a three-step financial plan:

- **Step One:** How much money do you have?
- **Step Two:** Where do you have it?
- **Step Three:** Let's move it to my company.

These financial advisors spend a lot of time trying to convince you that you need to move your money. They bring up products, stocks, and most inexcusably, average rates of return.

These brokers and salespeople are only interested in two things:

1. How much money you are going make (because a happy client is a good client)
2. How much money he or she is going to make

Make sure your advisor keeps the priority of how much *you* make, above how much he or she makes.

In recent years, the financial services industry has caught a lot of heat for bad and misleading practices. Arthur Levitt, the former head of the Securities and Exchange Commission (SEC), once said that "brokers are paid to buy and sell – not necessarily to look out for investors' best interests." Levitt also added that branch managers are part of the problem, because their compensation is based on selling products. He also said that the majority of brokers are not sufficiently trained to handle the wide variety of investment products they sell.

Remember the *Consumer Reports* story where the secret shopper went to five brokers? After going to two independent advisors and three big name brokerage houses, the secret shopper reported that the independents did a better job. And as you might expect, independent brokers don't have branch managers. You can begin to see why the independents had better ratings.

Investors have become understandably angry as they've learned the truth about Wall Street racketeering. Critics say that during the bull market analysts and their firms had a powerful incentive to issue overly optimistic reports about many of the stocks they covered. In many cases, these firms had already collected huge fees by selling the companies' stock to the public and stood to collect even more in fees if the price of the stock remained high.

We've already learned that unbiased recommendations were a myth in the late 1990's. And even today, how many "buy" recommendations do you hear about and see...versus "sell" recommendations? It's still pretty lopsided.

So, while firms and analysts profited handsomely from these fees, investors who followed the advice of their firm's analysts fared poorly. A lot of retired investors fared poorly over the last few years because of their broker's advice, and that probably applies to you as well.

And now that you realize all of this, **it's in your best interest to look for someone who is the opposite of these brokers and salespeople**.

The good always takes care of itself, so be more concerned with the possible downside to your investments. This may sound pessimistic, but you need to look at the worst case scenarios that may arise in your life. If you are prepared to deal with your worst case scenario, anything else will be easy.

But how do most brokers and salespeople address the downside? Not surprisingly, most don't. Here's how the majority of investors were informed about the potential downside to their investments:

Brokers typically spend several one-hour sessions telling the investor how great a particular investment is and how much money they stand to make from it. Once they have sufficiently explained the product and gotten the investor excited, they simply mention a quick caveat that reminds them that nothing is guaranteed. Usually it goes something like, "Now there are no guarantees about this, but if the market goes down and you hold it long enough, it should take care of itself."

That's it. Those two sentences are how the majority of brokers in this country address the downside of any investment. If that's the best they can say, do you really think they have your best interests at heart?

At this point in your life, you already have a comfortable retirement. Why risk it all by ignoring the worst case scenario that could happen to you? Most of us believe in Murphy's Law, and many of us count on the worst case scenario coming true at some point. I want to be prepared for the worst thing that can happen to me and my family, because if I can live with that, everything else will take care of itself – and your investments should be handled the same way.

As an investor, you should be looking for an advisor who is willing to tell you in detail the worst that could happen. If an advisor says to you, "Here's the worst thing that could happen. Can you live with that?" then you've found a professional who truly has your best interests at heart.

SLOW AND STEADY WINS THE RACE

When does −30 + 43 = 0? When you are looking at the return of your investments, that's when. If you own an investment that loses 30% of its value, you'll need to make 43% the following year just to break even. In fact, if you have $100 and lose 50%, you've got $50, right? Well, in order to get back your original $100, you'd have to make 100%, or double your money (double the remaining $50), the following year.

HOW DOES A LOSS AFFECT RETIRED FOLKS?

According to an October 2011 Time/Money Magazine poll, 77% of individuals between the ages of 50 and 70 who own investments indicated that they lost money in either individual stocks, mutual funds, or other investment accounts during 2007-2008. Worse yet, the majority of those individuals were forced to make lifestyle changes due to their investment losses.

Adjustments Made to Lifestyle Due to Losses	Percentage of Those Who Lost Money
Used College or Retirement savings to pay bills	40%
Borrowed money from family to pay bills	29%
Took fewer vacations	70%
Postponed a major purchase	50%
Had difficulty paying for health- care or prescription drugs	27%

You can see that when you take a hit, it takes an awful lot of effort just to get back to where you started. Worse yet, this doesn't even mention the loss of time. When something like this happens, you've lost the opportunity to make money and you lose the time it takes just to get back to even. No one should want to take unnecessary risks.

Let's say that I'm going to race you for a comfortable retirement, and I have two cars for us. Since I'm such a nice guy, I'm going to allow you to choose which car you want to drive. The first car has seat belts, reinforced doors, a fire extinguisher, and air bags, but can only go 80 mph. The other car has no safety equipment, is made with lots of plastic, is very light, and can go 140 mph.

You can choose a slower car that will withstand an 80 mph crash into a brick wall and allow you to walk away unscathed. Or you can choose a faster car that will zip along at 140 mph, but may easily flip and will rip apart like paper if you have an accident. Which do you want to drive?

The slower car, of course! But you are more likely to win with the faster car...so why would anyone choose a car they know is slower in this situation? Because it's safe.

Now, what if you could participate in stocks without any market risk? There is a particular technique that works a lot like the crash-proof car. It gets you where you want to be, but you can't crash and get hurt. It's a new hybrid technique that's been around for just over 10 years, and it's perfect for people who don't want to take any risk but still want stock market-like returns. It's a great option for every senior investor in the country.

CHAPTER 9

WHAT IS IT YOU WANT YOUR PORTFOLIO TO DO?

I N THE POLL REPORTED ON by AARP, 61% of people aged 44 to 75 said they feared depleting their savings *more* than they feared dying. It's an amazing statistic when you consider that this phenomenon is relatively new; people haven't always been this afraid of living.

So, what changed?

You can probably point to three things that have people unnerved: First, we're living a lot longer. Second, there are fewer guarantees. And third, the future just doesn't feel quite as bright.

If you are in your mid 60's (the age most people look to retire) your average life expectancy is 85...

> Death may be frightening, but to a majority of older Americans, the possibility of outliving their savings is even worse.
>
> -- CAROL FLECK *AARP BULLETIN JULY 1, 2010*

with a good chance that if you are married, one or the other of you will live past age 90. That means your retirement savings may have to last 25 years or more.

And that's at a time when pensions have largely gone away. There just aren't the same kinds of guarantees and safety nets there used to be for people who retire. Even Social Security (one of the few guarantees left for most people) is under constant scrutiny and attack.

The markets and the economy certainly haven't helped either. Long-term problems like the deficit, European debt, high gas prices, and skyrocketing healthcare costs tend to weigh down the markets. So, older Americans are right to be concerned about their financial futures.

How do you retire and make your money last given all the obstacles?

WHAT WORKED THEN DOESN'T WORK NOW

It comes down to income; while you were working you had a paycheck. But how do you replace that paycheck in retirement?

One idea from the past was to take income from a bond portfolio. Bonds were generally considered safe as long as you held them to maturity. And they paid a fixed rate of interest that you could use as reliable and predictable income.

Most advisors don't recommend this strategy anymore, and it's easy to see why:

Imagine you needed $40,000 per year to live comfortably and bonds were paying 5%. How much would you have to put in bonds to generate an annual income of $40,000?

That's an easy question for a financial planner. You'd have to put $800,000 into that kind of a bond portfolio ($40,000 divided by 5%).

But that's a lot to allocate to bonds (even if you have the money). And more importantly, the income doesn't go up with inflation.

With people living longer and healthcare costs rising exponentially it doesn't take long for inflation to overwhelm the "paycheck" you get from bonds. It's a strategy that doesn't work when people retire early and live a long time.

But it's a strategy that worked when people retired at 65 and only had a life expectancy to age 72. If you were only going to be retired for 6 or 7 years then you didn't have to worry about inflation.

Relying on bonds for retirement income is an example of something that used to work but doesn't work any longer because the retirement landscape has changed so dramatically in the last few years. People live a lot longer and have to rely a lot more on their personal savings.

Living longer means inflation has become a very real problem; and it's a problem that bonds can't solve.

WHAT WORKS NOW MAY NOT WORK FOR LONG

Growth is the only way to combat inflation, and historically there is no better place to grow your money than in the stock market. Financial professionals are convinced that a stock portfolio is the best way to grow your money to stay ahead of inflation.

A typical investor's portfolio is stock-heavy to maximize growth (with a few bonds sprinkled in to smooth out any temporary losses). These "balanced" portfolios adjust as the years go by to include more bonds as a person ages. But even after rebalancing, these portfolios continue to hold half or more of their assets in stocks for growth.

The idea is that you can safely withdraw 4% from that kind of portfolio (growing with inflation) in retirement and never run out of money.

That strategy worked through the decade of the 90's and is still used today to draw income in retirement. In theory, you are pulling money from a combination of interest, dividends, and capital gains. And as long as the markets cooperate you'll be fine.

As long as the markets cooperate.

There lies the problem. The markets don't always cooperate. There are years when both stocks and bonds are down...it's something we know to be true from our experience with the markets in the last 10 years.

And if you don't have interest, dividends, or capital gains to pull from...and you still need the "paycheck"...you have to withdraw it from your principal.

And that's when you run the very real risk of running out of money.

WHAT KIND OF MARKET ARE WE IN?

It's a risk that is a lot more real than most advisors care to admit. Why? They just don't have any experience with today's problems.

Consider this:

Most advisors are in their late 40's or early 50's. If we just take age 50 as a reasonable average, the typical advisor was born around 1960. Assuming they graduated college, they entered the workforce around 1982 (age 22).

What were the markets like for the next 18 years?

Look at the graph:

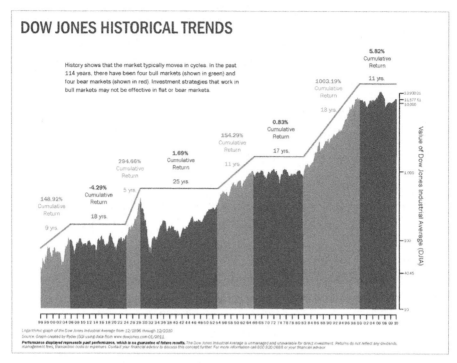

DOW JONES HISTORICAL TRENDS

History shows that the market typically moves in cycles. In the past 114 years, there have been four bull markets (shown in green) and four bear markets (shown in red). Investment strategies that work in bull markets may not be effective in flat or bear markets.

From 1982 to 2000 the market was straight up...and people were making a lot of money in nearly every stock or mutual fund they invested in. Sure, there were occasional dips in performance, but if you simply sat tight and did nothing you recovered and continued to grow your money.

What was the best financial advice at that time? Buy stocks and hold them through the downturns; you can't go wrong!

And for most advisors, that's the bulk of their experience. They still generally stick to that advice.

But look at the market immediately preceding 1982...the 17 year period between 1965 and 1981. The cumulative return during that entire 17 year period was only 0.83 percent!

The graph shows that those kinds of markets are not anomalies. They happen, and they last a long time.

If you had to guess what kind of market we are in now, would you say we are in another bull market like we saw through the '80's and '90's, or do you think we are closer to the uncertain markets we saw in the '70's?

It's an entirely different time with an entirely different set of problems. And it requires completely different ideas and different advice, especially if you are retired or retiring.

The problem is that if your savings are predominantly in equities and you rely on those savings to draw a "paycheck," a market like we've seen this past decade doesn't allow you to withdraw 4% per year.

Ideally you would have withdrawn a cumulative 40% from the beginning of 2000 through the end of 2009 (4% per year for 10 years). The graph shows that the cumulative return during that entire decade was only 5.82 percent! That's cumulative...for the entire decade...not the annual average rate of return.

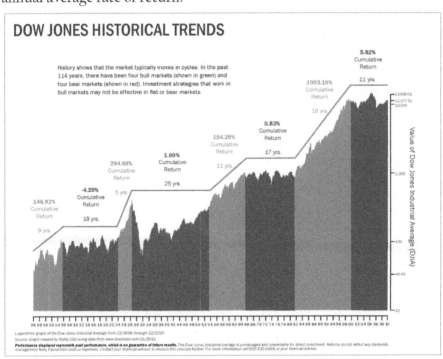

DOW JONES HISTORICAL TRENDS

History shows that the market typically moves in cycles. In the past 114 years, there have been four bull markets (shown in green) and four bear markets (shown in red). Investment strategies that work in bull markets may not be effective in flat or bear markets.

Logarithmic graph of the Dow Jones Industrial Average from 12/1896 through 12/2010

Source: Graph created by Rydex|SGI using data from www.djindexes.com 01/2011

Performance displayed represents past performance, which is no guarantee of future results. The Dow Jones Industrial Average is unmanaged and unavailable for direct investment. Returns do not reflect any dividends, management fees, transaction costs or expenses. Contact your financial advisor to discuss this concept further. For more information call 800.820.0888 or your financial advisor.

It isn't that there aren't any years in which you could withdraw 4%, it's just that there are too many years where you can't; you end up drawing from principal. And by doing that you absolutely run a risk of running out of money the longer you live.

For many people who retired in the early 2000's the reality of that happening is beginning to sink in. It's why 61% of them responded that they fear outliving their assets more than they fear dying.

WHAT'S THE SOLUTION?

There is an obvious fix for all of this: "Don't take money in down years".... or at least take less. But that's really not an option for the vast majority of people. They need a paycheck to live. And they can't afford to take a 50% pay cut for a couple of years while their accounts recover...or worse, go without income at all for that period of time.

Bonds don't work because inflation eventually overwhelms an income that doesn't grow. And a stock-heavy portfolio sprinkled with a few bonds doesn't work because you need income each and every year...even years when the market is down. So, what can you do?

An idea that emerged from many of the country's leading business schools was a modified form of asset laddering.

The idea of asset laddering was something that had been around a long time. Many of us are familiar with (or have at least heard of) laddering CD's or bonds.

I'm not going to go into the ins and outs of laddering, but essentially laddering was an attempt to increase the yields on fixed-rate investments to overcome the obvious inflation problem as people began living longer. Laddering also sought to ease the interest rate sensitivity of bonds by having shorter term bonds in the front part of the ladder. By laddering, people could buy bonds or CD's with longer maturities that paid higher yields while still minimizing the risk of loss due to interest rate sensitivity.

It helped, but it didn't really solve the two biggest problems inherent in bonds:

First, things like health care and food (because of oil prices and transportation costs) tend to rise a lot faster than the government's official inflation rate. So, the higher yields still didn't make a dent in the kind of inflation most retirees experience.

Second, there was still the problem of the amount of money you needed to allocate to bonds to start with. Remember our rather modest income of $40,000? It required us to allocate $800,000 to bonds in a 5% interest rate environment (more if interest rates were lower). That's an awful lot to allocate to fixed assets.

THE EVOLUTION OF AN IDEA

But in 1997 a group of graduate students working on their MBA at the University of San Francisco began looking at ways to modify laddering. That research resulted in a lengthy white paper entitled "Asset Dedication".

The concept that emerged was something they called "bond bridging". It introduced two novel ideas:

The first idea was to add equities into the laddering equation. Before this, it was assumed that equities couldn't be laddered because the returns were uncertain and unreliable; there would be gains, but there would also be losses.

The second idea was that a mix of fixed investments (some bonds... some "not bonds") could be laddered and *spent down to zero* as an income "bridge" to the growth and equities side of the portfolio.

It's not my intention to go into the math or academic theory behind the idea of "bond bridging". I only bring it up to make the point that the idea was a real improvement on the laddering concept.

Introducing equities in the ladder and using a mix of fixed investments that included bonds and "not bonds" seemed to solve the problem of inflation.

And spending the fixed portion of the portfolio to zero (not just spending fixed interest) substantially reduced the initial investment someone would have to make in fixed assets to get the income they were looking for.

It's too bad the paper came out in the late '90's. The stock market was booming and not many people outside of academia took notice.

BUT COULD IT WORK?

A debate inside the halls of this country's leading business schools broke out over the merits of "bond bridging". And when the dust settled the consensus was that "bond bridging" would work, but that it might not be necessary.

Let me explain:

"Bond bridging" advocates argued that you could withdraw more money as a result of structuring your portfolio this way.

They also argued that the "bond bridge" would provide virtually guaranteed income for the first 5 years of withdrawals which would get someone to the equities side of the portfolio where they could reallocate some of the growth of that money to create another "bond bridge" of income for the next 5 years.

It's important to note that no one came out and said, "You shouldn't do this." All they said was, "it might not be necessary". Their argument went something like this:

It's true that the first 5 years of income would be virtually guaranteed. And that would "bridge" someone to the growth side of the portfolio (which would presumably have grown during those 5 years). Having the equities on the back side of the ladder is a good idea since even if there were down years the account would have time to recover. But, 5 years may not be enough time to recover. Most times it will be. But there are scenarios where it won't. People may be lulled into a false sense of security that it will always work when, in actuality, it might only work "most of the time".

Second, the sum of the parts can't be more than the whole. If, for example, you ladder 50% of the assets in the income bridge and ladder the remaining 50% of the assets to growth; the performance of that portfolio will be the same as a conventional 50/50 balanced portfolio. The income you would generate couldn't be more than the income that the 50/50 portfolio could generate. It's ultimately unnecessary to do this.

Remember, this was the late '90's when the stock market was booming, and a lot of financial professionals weren't looking for a solution to a problem that didn't exist. At the time, no one ever imagined there would be a year (much less "years") when you couldn't take 4% from any kind of stock portfolio.

The naysayers were right and they were wrong. I'll explain in a minute, but for now it's only important to note that while no reasons emerged not to do this, it was clear that the idea could be improved.

THE CADILLAC OF RETIREMENT PLANS

Advocates of "bond bridging" went to work right away to improve it. The result is something I call the Smart Asset Income Ladder...or SAIL for short.

How does it work?

It improves on the improvements that "bond bridging" made to the laddering concept. It's a ladder that like "bond bridging:"

- Includes stocks and other growth assets as part of the ladder
- Is structured to spend the income assets to zero as a bridge to the growth assets

But it's improved to:

- Extend the bridge to a 10 year time horizon
- Efficiently leverage the "non-bond" concept original to "bond bridging" so that it's not even necessary to change any of your investments. You can simply take what you already have and restructure it in a mathematical ladder.

Let's look at an example:

Suppose you had a $300,000 portfolio and you needed to supplement your Social Security in retirement. Most advisors would tell you that as long as the markets cooperate you can safely take out $12,000 (4%) each year.

But what if the markets don't cooperate? What if you're caught in a choppy and volatile market?

If you find yourself in that kind of market, there will be years when your advisor will recommend that you take less than $12,000...or even suggest you take no income at all until your accounts recover.

However, by using the SAIL concept, not only can you safely pull out your needed income...you can pull out more than $12,000 safely.

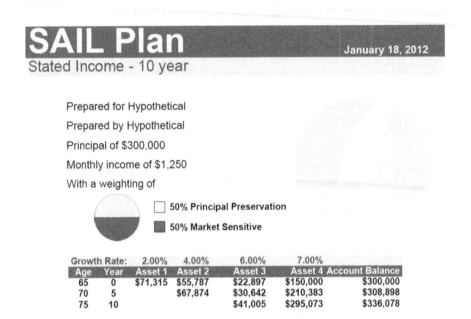

SAIL Plan

January 18, 2012

Stated Income - 10 year

Prepared for Hypothetical

Prepared by Hypothetical

Principal of $300,000

Monthly income of $1,250

With a weighting of

☐ 50% Principal Preservation

■ 50% Market Sensitive

Growth Rate:	2.00%	4.00%	6.00%	7.00%	
Age	Year	Asset 1	Asset 2	Asset 3	Asset 4	Account Balance
65	0	$71,315	$55,787	$22,897	$150,000	$300,000
70	5		$67,874	$30,642	$210,383	$308,898
75	10			$41,005	$295,073	$336,078

This isn't complicated or costly to do. Remember, one of the improvements of SAIL was that you don't have to change any of your investments; you just have to organize them the way the SAIL calculator suggests.

It's the same $300,000 invested the same way. But notice you are getting $1,250 per month. That's $15,000 per year...a significant improvement over the $12,000 most advisors would recommend.

In addition, that $15,000 is guaranteed for 10 years. Regardless of how choppy or volatile the markets get, you never have to take a pay cut or go without income.

IS SAIL REALLY NECESSARY?

"Bond bridging" didn't have any real critics. But, remember, many financial professionals liked to point out that it might not be necessary.

If you don't have to change any of your investments, why can't you take the same $15,000 from the 50/50 portfolio that every other advisor would recommend?

Remember, I noted that the naysayers were right and they were wrong. They were right in the sense that the sum of the parts isn't necessarily more than the whole. In *hindsight*, they *might* have been able to withdraw $15,000 per year from the 50/50 portfolio.

But only in hindsight (in other words, they would never have recommended you start the first couple of years that way), and you still might have had to take a pay cut in a non-SAIL portfolio somewhere along the way. Here's why:

The front part of the SAIL plan guarantees your income for the first 10 years. In this case, you are assured of 10 years of $15,000 per year income...*but only because you are spending the front part of the plan to zero.* You are comfortable doing that because it's a **bridge** to the back part of the plan where your assets are growing to replace (and even exceed) your original investment.

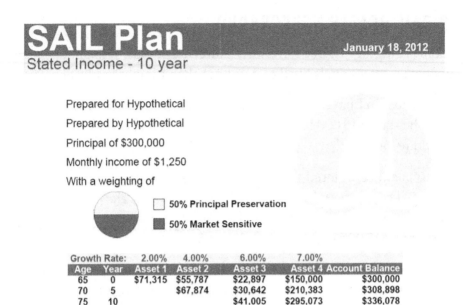

In a conventional 50/50 portfolio you wouldn't be able to withdraw your $15,000 in a year when the market was down.

The reason is that your advisor isn't planning on spending *any* assets in the portfolio down to zero. Instead, he's relying on your income coming from the interest and capital gains inside the portfolio. So, what does he recommend you do in a year where there is a loss or insufficient growth?

He recommends that you take less income or he recommends that you don't take any income until your portfolio recovers; you end up taking a pay cut for a period of time (sometimes years).

Your advisor knows that if you start spending principal to make up the income gap in down years you could end up in a death spiral:

- You lock in losses and reduce your principal

- Which reduces the amount of interest in future years (because of the reduced principal)...

- Making it necessary to dip into principal again the following year...

- Which reduces your principal

- Which reduces the amount of interest in future years...

You get the point. Advisors counsel their clients not to do that. But they turn a blind-eye when the client (out of necessity) is forced to do it anyway. Advisors know that the effect of these withdrawals in down years will ripple as the client ages until the client realizes too late that they won't have enough money if they live too long. Remember the AARP poll?

THE DANGER OF USING A BALANCED PORTFOLIO

If you retired at the beginning of the year 2000 with $300,000 in retirement savings and withdrew $15,000 from a conventional 50/50 portfolio you would end up with an ending balance of $178,527 at the end of 2009.

At that point you would need to grow that portfolio by 8.4% each and every year just to maintain the $178,000 balance and still pull your $15,000 per year paycheck. Next time you sit down with your advisor, ask him what he thinks would happen if you withdrew 8 ½ percent from your portfolio each and every year. He will tell you that you will probably run out of money.

WHY DOESN'T THAT HAPPEN IN A SAIL PLAN?

Because of the math embedded in the SAIL calculator. The SAIL is essentially an income roadmap that tells you how to organize and systematically liquidate your slowest growing assets in sequence as a *bridge* to the growth assets.

Growth assets will sometimes lose money. But given enough time, they recover and grow...provided they are untouched during the recovery period. The SAIL ensures that you can take your income and still not tap into the growth assets during the recovery period.

In the typical 50/50 portfolio, your advisor can't liquidate any of your assets in down years because he doesn't know when the market will fall, how much it will fall, or how long it will take to recover. And, as we've seen, once you begin to liquidate assets you can't ever go back to just withdrawing interest because of the "death spiral" we looked at.

That's why a $300,000 account fell to $178,527 from 2000 through 2009...even though there were more years that the market did better than 4% than years where it fell short.

The best thing to do, then, is to **plan from the very beginning** to systematically spend down the income assets **in case** there are any down years. That way you are covered no matter what happens. That's what makes the "SAIL" concept so revolutionary.

The naysayers were right; you don't need this kind of plan when things are going great...it doesn't hurt, but it isn't necessary.

But you *do* need this kind of plan if things ever get unpredictable or choppy. The SAIL calculator makes it easy to mathematically construct an income plan that works in any kind of market!

SAIL Plan
Stated Income - 10 year
January 18, 2012

Prepared for Hypothetical

Prepared by Hypothetical

Principal of $300,000

Monthly income of $1,250

With a weighting of

☐ 50% Principal Preservation

■ 50% Market Sensitive

Growth Rate:	2.00%	4.00%	6.00%	7.00%	
Age	Year	Asset 1	Asset 2	Asset 3	Asset 4	Account Balance
65	0	$71,315	$55,787	$22,897	$150,000	$300,000
70	5		$67,874	$30,642	$210,383	$308,898
75	10			$41,005	$295,073	$336,078

IS TEN YEARS ENOUGH?

SAIL solves the problems people face when trying to replace their "paycheck" in retirement. And because there are no criticisms of SAIL everyone should at least look into it.

Only one question remains: Is ten years enough? Will a ten year time-frame be enough for down markets to recover? SAIL assumes that it will, but the extended downturn we're experiencing and downturns we've seen in the past mean we can't be positive.

Fortunately, the last three years have seen the development of special investments specifically designed to keep pace with inflation and provide a lifetime stream of income. The only catch? You need to be invested 10 years before turning on the income.

These special investments almost seem tailor-made for SAIL plans. If you are at (or approaching) retirement, I encourage you to seek out an advisor familiar with the SAIL concept and the accompanying "income investments" that have only recently appeared on the scene.

CHAPTER 10

WHAT IS IT YOU WANT YOUR PORTFOLIO TO DO?

THROUGHOUT THIS BOOK, WE'VE DISCUSSED a lot of options you and other retired investors can use to improve your financial situation. But before you begin putting these different ideas into action, you should take a few moments to prepare and decide how to best take advantage of your new knowledge.

As we've explained in previous chapters, each of the suggestions and techniques mentioned may or may not be appropriate for you. It's up to you to determine what will benefit you and what won't. Just as you should do a stress test of your current investments, you should also test out any changes to your portfolio before you actually make them.

WHAT SHOULD YOUR FINANCIAL PLAN LOOK LIKE?

We talked earlier about your financial situation being completely different from that of your children. And likewise, your financial needs may differ from your friends' and others. For example, a couple who continues to make a mortgage and car payment each month will need a different level of income than a couple whose home and cars are already paid for. An even better example is an individual who must pay for their spouse's long-term care costs, because the amount of income needed for these expenses is vastly greater than for an individual or couple who are in good health.

We all have different priorities, and your financial plan should reflect your unique situation. Unfortunately, most brokers and financial advisors use a cookie cutter, "one size fits all" approach. But rather than continuing to hold and invest in things someone else convinced you that you needed, you should begin evaluating things for yourself and determining what makes the most sense for you when it comes to your investments.

ANALYZE YOUR GOALS

The first step to changing your financial plan is analyzing your goals, since they will be the driving force behind everything you do. Most investors set goals for themselves when they first start out investing, but never update them to reflect the changes in their lives.

Worse yet, others simply start investing without any goals at all. At most, these individuals simply want to "make money." Yet making money isn't the goal of investing; making money is how you achieve your goals and dreams. Your goal may be to buy a second home in Florida and afford to travel back and forth between your houses each year. But making money on your investments is *how* you do that. Make sure your goals aren't about money, but what you will do with the money.

Now is the time to analyze your goals. If you are still chasing returns without consideration for income, then you need to change your goals to reflect your current financial needs and wants.

Are you looking to reduce taxes on your Social Security income? If so, you are going to look at different investments than someone who is simply looking for the next "big" stock. A review of your portfolio and taxes may tell you that you are paying a lot of taxes on money you aren't spending. In that situation, your needs are completely different from someone who is spending every cent they make.

ANALYZE YOUR PORTFOLIO

Once you've addressed your goals, it's time to look at your portfolio. Be sure to stress test each investment you own, as well as your overall holdings to see where you are at risk.

As you go through this step, see if you are covered for just about anything that might happen. Remember the worst case scenario: you should pose all sorts of questions and problems to see what could happen. In other words, don't just see what would happen if the market dips for 3 months or a year...take a look at what would happen over a prolonged 3-5 year dip.

Also, remember to ignore the "average" rate of return of your investments as you make these comparisons. You've already learned how this is not only misleading, but a big lie. So instead of saying, "Oh, this makes an average return of 12%, we're fine," compare your investments to an appropriate benchmark.

Using a proper benchmark is the key to making any improvement to your investments. Doing a financial stress test means not just looking at investments but reviewing your tax return every year, having your accounts and beneficiaries reviewed for correct titling and designation, and reviewing your legal affairs annually. All this may seem like a lot of work and a headache, but if you don't do it your financial plan will go right down the tubes.

If you go to the doctor with a headache, he doesn't give you an aspirin and send you home. He gives you a series of tests to see what the problem could be. It could be a tumor, an aneurysm, or a stroke, but the only way of knowing is by conducting tests. Your finances should be handled the same way.

In fact, if a doctor sent you home with an aspirin and you had a stroke, what would happen to that doctor? He'd lose his license. So if your advisor tries to tell you everything's fine and pushes you out the door, it's time to find a new advisor.

DO THEY MATCH?

Once you've gone through both your goals and your current portfolio, it's time to see how well they match. If you've done a good job stress testing your investments, you've probably found a few surprises that you want to fix. If so, don't be upset. After all, better to find out now than once it becomes a problem.

For example, you may learn that your mutual funds are geared toward accumulating wealth, and you've been losing some money over the past couple of years. This does not help you achieve your goal having enough income to live comfortably without the worry of running out of money. In order to achieve this, you need to be preserving what you have, not risking it to get more. You should also be running your portfolio through the SAIL calculator to give you the highest possible guaranteed income.

Likewise, you may have learned that you are paying a lot of taxes on money you aren't spending. Of course, if you didn't know you were giving all that extra money to Uncle Sam to begin with, you probably didn't arrange your portfolio to minimize your taxes.

By doing this, you match your goals and investments so they can work together to give you peace of mind and keep the money you've worked so hard to earn!

But now that you've found some of these problems with your portfolio (and realized that they don't match your goals) you have to ask yourself, "Why didn't my advisor already tell me this?"

For many people, the vast difference between their goals and the investments they hold lets them know that it's time for a new advisor – one that will put their needs first. Are you one of those people?

WHAT SHOULD YOU DO NOW?

The answer is, "A lot."

First, you need to decide whether or not to change advisors. Only you know the answer to that. But at this point, you should have a strong idea whether your advisor has simply missed a few things or cares more about lining his or her own pockets than looking out for you.

The things you've learned from this book should be a pretty good indicator. In fact, the more you've learned, the more you probably realize that there is a lot your advisor doesn't know. But if you've already heard everything in this book from your advisor, give yourself a pat on the back. Because if so, you are getting your money's worth, no matter what he or she is charging.

Next, you can act on the investments and ideas you've learned about. Talk to your advisor about the things in this book that most interest you, and get more information about other options that will help you achieve your goals. Don't feel that you have to do it all in one sitting, but begin by fixing the biggest problem with your portfolio or the one that bothers you the most.

The topics discussed in this book can literally save you thousands of dollars. Even if you act on just two or three of the techniques and ideas mentioned, they could be worth anywhere from $1,000 in the next few months to over $300,000 over time. And once you start making these changes, you'll see the improvements they can make. Eventually, you'll wonder why you hadn't taken these easy steps years ago.

CAN YOU HAVE YOUR CAKE AND EAT IT TOO?

Absolutely. In fact, by reading this book you've already learned how to do it.

If you ask retirees who have used the information in this book how their portfolio is doing, they will almost always tell you that they are doing all the things they've always dreamed of without losing a wink of sleep. And that's the best answer anyone can give.

Retired folks who have leveraged the things we've talked about in the book are:

- Paying less taxes on their Social Security income

- No longer at risk of accidentally disinheriting their grandchildren

- Paying little or no tax on money they aren't spending

- Have increased their monthly income significantly while at the same time eliminating their chance of running out of money

- Have peace of mind...and isn't that the real goal of retirement?

I wish you good luck and a wonderful retirement!

FPO

ENDNOTES

1   Source: 2011 Investment Company Fact Book

2   Source: CBS News

3   Source: 2009 Investopedia.com via Morning Star

4   Source: Genworth 2001 Cost of Care Survey

5   Source: www.efmoody.com

6   Source: www.aaltci.org

7   Source: October 2010 Minnesota House of Representatives Brief

8   Source: Principals of Macroeconomics, Gregory Mankiw

9   Source: www.FDIC.gov

10 Source: www.FDIC.gov

Made in the USA
Columbia, SC
17 July 2018